W9-BKN-270

Keeping the Spirit of Christmas

Christmas Day

An Acrostic by

WALTER RIDYARD

C hristmas Day to Christians dear,
H appiest day of all the year;
R ejoice we all with one accord,
I n worshipping our Infant Lord;
S on of God in helpless state,
T he Son of Man, God Incarnate
M eanly housed in cattle stall,
A cclaimed by Angels, Lord of all,
S aviour of a fallen race.

D ivinely stooping to embrace
A ll and sundry, whosoever
Y ield themselves to Love's endeavour.

Keeping the Spirit of Christmas

by

HANDEL H. BROWN

Pastor of the First Presbyterian Church
St. Cloud, Florida

William B. Eerdmans Publishing Company
Grand Rapids, Michigan

Library of Congress Catalog Card Number, 65-25183

I dedicate this book
to the memory of my Bahamian father-in-law

ALBERT E. PINDER
1892 — 1960

a humble servant of God
a wise and beloved leader of his people
who welcomed me into his family
and enriched my ministry with encouragement

Foreword

This is my third Christmas book. Although I have included material which continues where *When Jesus Came* leaves off, this is an independent volume, with its own special emphases.

The two themes I have sought to stress are the Centrality of Jesus and the Universality of the Christmas Message. This has involved a certain amount of repetition, but as this has always been an accepted method of teaching, and as the repetition has been reduced to a minimum, I do not think it is necessary to apologize for it.

Again, I want to express my gratitude to my wife Dollie, whose devotion and care made it possible for me to write this book.

—HANDEL H. BROWN

St. Cloud, Florida

Contents

PROLOGUE

Getting Ready for Christmas

CHILDREN ARE NOT THE ONLY PEOPLE WHO ASK QUESTIONS at Christmas time. Grown-ups ask them too. Thinking men and women cannot face this blessed season without struggling violently with some of life's greatest problems.

This is as it should be. If we are to prepare ourselves spiritually for the Advent Festival, we must use the minds God has given us to think about it in a serious manner.

The nature of Christmas thrusts upon us questions which, at other times, we successfully evade. It is the happiest time of the entire year. It is also the most wasteful season. We put aside our calculators and our computers. We forget all about such things as budgets and thrift. We are lavish in our expenditures. We want our gifts to bring as much pleasure as possible to our loved-ones. For once, the table must groan under an unnecessary weight of unaccustomed delicacies.

We go out of our way to show a friendly approach. We call it "the Christmas spirit." We not only sing about goodwill, we try to practice what we sing. A feeling of carefree happiness envelopes us. We rejoice in our peace and plenty.

We do all this in a world which is perched precariously on the edge of an abominable abyss. There is trouble wherever we look. Cuba is not unique in the Western Hemisphere. What about Panama? Would you choose to live in South America? If you have investments in any of those Republics, you know how unstable they are. On the other side of the globe, the invasion of India by Red China has lost the headlines. Yet it is related to far more than Laos, Viet Nam, and Cambodia, and we have not heard the last of it. From one end of Africa to the other, the native populations are either "seething with the ugly spirit of rebellion" or "bursting with noble aspirations," depending on which way you look at them.

We can always find specious explanations. It is easy to say that agitators and mischief-makers are exploiting unrest for their own evil purposes. It is probably true so far as it goes, but we cannot leave it at that. It does not touch the basic question: Why is there unrest in these countries in the first place?

If we fail to ask this question, we shall not be able to get things in perspective. We are stupid indeed if we imagine we can stick the label "Communism" on every trouble spot, and think we have diagnosed the malady. If we probe far enough we shall discover that Communism is only a symptom and that the disease lies much deeper. We often lose sight of the fact that Communism claims to be the *remedy* for all the economic, sociological, and political ills of mankind.

Not long ago, a visitor to the Far East was approached by a hungry man who said, "If my family had one can of your American dog food a week, we should think we were fortunate people." Tell this to your festive friends while you are eating your sumptuous Christmas dinner. It may not be pleasant to talk about such things under such circumstances, but we are culpable if we ignore them. Taste is a poor standard of truth.

Outbursts of violence in different parts of the world today are not necessarily *inspired* by a foreign political party with a fallacious and insidious ideology. No doubt this party *encourages* and *aids* them, but people have always rioted when they were starving. They always will. What have they to lose?

Other rebellions are caused by oppression and exploitation. It is a sad commentary on our mental processes that we who live in the racially troubled South often fail to see that we are only reaping what we have sown. The Principle of Justice is implanted in the soul of every man. It is bound to demand recognition, one way or another.

It is not our task to condemn these rebellious movements out of hand. Rather, we must seek to understand them. When men realize that there is such a thing as "Right," then, sooner or later, they will resist cruelty and tyranny. Unfortunately, it so happens that often the only way open to the oppressed is the wrong way of bloodshed, lawlessness, and hate.

It is not a pleasant experience to face up to the harsh realities of life at Christmas time, but face up to them we must. In the light of distressing conditions which are apparent on every side today, let us ask again some old questions. Is there a God, or is our world the result of chance? If there is a God, has He anything to do with Christmas? If we can associate this God with Christmas, does that mean He is in any way like the Babe whose birth we celebrate, and the Man He grew up to be? How can we know whether Christmas is real or spurious?

Christianity is not a subject you can study in College. It is not like logic, geometry or physics. You can learn *about* it, but the strangest paradox of the Gospel is just this: if you want to know whether it is true or not, you have to accept it first. This sounds like putting the cart before the horse, but unless you accept Jesus Himself as your Lord and Saviour, the answer is not there. "The natural man receiveth not the things of the Spirit of God: for they are foolishness unto him: neither can he know them, because they are spiritually discerned" (1 Corinthians 2:14). Only those who "taste and see" know that "the Lord is good." This is one field in which experience must precede knowledge. The qualified judge of religious truth is not the critic but the saint. Christian doctrine did not produce Christian experience. It was the other way around. "That . . . which we have heard, which we have seen with our eyes, which we have looked upon, and our hands have handled, of the Word of life . . . that which we have seen and heard declare we unto you" (1 John 1:1f.).

The meaning and the goal of our existence are discerned in Jesus. Not in what He *says* so much as in what He *is,* and in what He becomes to those who love Him. We have to know Him before we can know the answers.

This is not a denial of the place of reason in religion. It is the assertion that reason, *by itself,* is inadequate. I repeat what I said earlier: we must use the minds God has given us, to think in a serious manner. But until we think *as Christians,* the answer will evade us.

* * * * *

The Festival of our Lord's birth is an occasion for throwing the glory of His Incarnation across the dark shadows of our perplexity. God manifest in the flesh is a mighty and surpassing mystery. Our deepest thoughts about it are mere glimpses of its outer garments. Yet it has been the essential faith of all the Christian ages.

To prepare ourselves for this glad season, we must kneel and worship, and, in that humble spirit, we must wrestle with the incongruities of life. For then Love will lead the mind. Then we can walk with the Shepherds and the Wise Men, trusting that at last, through love and loyalty, we shall be brought, like them, to the light we seek.

O God! the pure alone, —
E'en in their deep confessing, —
Can see Thee as their own,
And find the perfect blessing;
Yet to each waiting soul
Speak in Thy still small voice,
Till broken love's made whole,
And saddened hearts rejoice.

—J. Martineau

Ours is an age of a lot of noise and very little light. A prevalent heresy is the foolish notion that the loudest word carries farthest and lives longest. Noise is especially characteristic of those who would have us believe theirs is the *only* way. There is so much that blares at us today that it is becoming increasingly difficult to find the light, to know the truth, and to make responsible individual judgments.

There is a beautiful contrast between light and noise. You watch the sun rising in the east, quietly stealing into the sky, dispelling the night, and gently waking all nature to life and loveliness. It does not shout. It does not cry aloud. It moves silently across the world, transforming it.

And so it is with Jesus. He is not the Big Noise that shatters our individual judgment. He is the Light which enables us to see things more clearly, and to exercise our discernment more intelligently. "In Thy light we see light."

We are bewildered as we ponder our gross human situation. We ask God, Why? His clearest answer comes, not in the form of a logical syllogism, not as a mathematical formula, but in the form of a Son. He whispers to our seeking hearts, "I am the Way" (John 14:6). Despite our limitations, when we accept Him as the Way, we discover, to our joy, that He is also the Light. We do not rise to spiritual heights by pouring over self-improvement guidebooks, but by sitting at His feet.

We must be willing, here also, to "become as little children," so that we might "enter the kingdom of God" (Matthew 18:3). The gracious invitation of Jesus still stands, "Come unto me . . . take my yoke upon you, and learn of me" (Matthew 11:28f.). The "coming" must precede the "learning." We do not realize the depth of our ignorance until we humbly come to Him. No pride can come to Him.

A man who was puffed up with a false sense of his own importance picked a quarrel with a fellow deacon of the church. He followed him into the sanctuary. He sat through the worship service so that as soon as the benediction was pronounced he could renew the quarrel and, as he put it, "let him know who it was he was dealing with." We learn by painful experience that there is a religion which is not Christ's religion.

No spirit of "I know it all" can worship at the Manger. Such an attitude always does irreparable harm to the Kingdom.

No pride can stand before Him. No spirit of "I know it all" can be His disciple. Except we become as little children and acknowledge Him as our Lord, Master, Saviour, Example, and Friend, we are none of His. He who calls us to be as little children, Himself became a humble Child.

Humility was not first brought to birth in that stable at Bethlehem. It became incarnate there. Its reign was already from of old, when the morning stars sang together. Humility is not a mask worn by weakness. It was a sword in the hand of Michael when Lucifer was thrust down from heaven.

Humility is the spirit in which, from Creation's earliest dawn, the Divine finger has awakened all things into life. It is the spirit in which a bounteous Providence, beholding all things that are in heaven and on earth, has crowned the year with His goodness.

Humility is the spirit in which the heavenly Father has wistfully sought the love and friendship of His children. It is not the creation of His hand. It lives in the beating of His heart. It was personified on earth in Him who, "being in the form of God, thought it not robbery to be equal with God: but made himself of no reputation, and took upon him the form of a servant, and was made in the likeness of men: and being found in fashion as a man, he humbled himself, and became obedient unto death, even the death of the cross" (Philippians 2:6ff.).

He it was who said, "Be ye therefore perfect, even as your Father which is in heaven is perfect" (Matthew 5:48). Only in the hallowed fellowship of Jesus can this miracle be wrought. Only as we know Him are we brought to the place where we can see with the eye of faith, for, in the last analysis, only love can open the inward eye. Only love can remove the scales. "Through love to light."

Christ freely offers His friendship to everyone. Not only is none excluded, but none is preferred. His overture embraces all. It is in His fellowship that we grow in Grace and in the knowledge of His Will, because it is in fellowship that love deepens.

Miracles happen in Christ's school. The dullest pupil makes progress. The most gloomy and morbid doubter begins to believe. The most wavering and unstable follower is strengthened. In His fellowship, darkness gives way to light.

* * * * *

We fail to get ready for Christmas because we have lost the spirit of expectancy. We have become so conventional about even so great a Feast as this that we do not expect Jesus to be present at His own birthday party.

A little refugee boy, five years old, was taken by his foster-parents to the toy carnival in a huge department store. It was his first visit to the enchanted land. His eyes popped open wide and glistened with excitement. After a while he began to look under the tables, and to search behind the counters. His foster-parents and the store-clerks wondered what he was looking for. Then he stammered, "But where is the Baby Jesus?" Thousands of eager shoppers visited that store daily. How many of them expected to see Jesus there?

Christmas has lost its meaning for us because we have lost the spirit of expectancy. We cannot prepare our hearts for an *observance*. We need to prepare them for an *experience*.

The Christmas experience is not something we can "work up" by our own enthusiasm or by the diligence we put into our preparations for Christmas. It is something we can have only by God's help and inspiration. We do not manufacture the Christmas spirit for ourselves. It is derived from somewhere. There is a Source from which it flows.

God is the Source of the Christmas spirit. It is His gift, and it has to be received. It cannot be achieved. It cannot be received in a vacuum. It is bound up with Shepherds, Wise Men, a Star, Angels, a Song, and, most important, a helpless tiny Babe who is God's Love Gift to this loveless world.

To prepare our hearts for Christmas, we must cultivate the spirit of expectancy.

Have you ever realized what a stir that first Christmas caused? We talk so much about the coming of God being "unnoticed" that we are in danger of losing our perspective. His own people "knew him not" (John 1:11), but what about the others?

On the national scene, the Edomite King Herod was so disturbed that he ordered his soldiers to take their swords and murder all the little children they could find in Bethlehem. "He was troubled, and all Jerusalem with him" (Matthew 2:3). It was almost a state of national emergency. Do we expect Christmas to impinge upon our nation?

On the international scene, the first Christmas had repercussions as far away as Persia or Babylon. There, Wise Men gathered together their most costly treasures, and dashed across the desert to offer them to the Child. Do we expect any significant pagan acknowledgment of His birth?

This birth caused a stir, not only on earth, but in the limitless regions of Outer Space. The very heavens were aflame with constellations. They resounded to the strains of a choir which was unique. Seraphic songs, unheard before, announced His glory.

He spake, and straightway the celestial choir
In hymns of joy, unknown before, conspire.
The praises of redeeming love they sang,
And heaven's whole orb with hallelujahs rang.

—John Byrom

Christmas was the greatest thing that had ever happened. When we realize this, we shall begin to recover the spirit of expectancy. We shall begin to expect it to be of more than passing interest to us. We shall begin to expect to see God, and His Eternal Purpose, in it.

If we are to get ready for Christmas, we must try to understand the purpose of our Holy Saviour's birth. Jesus was born into this finite world so that we might become true children of God, with all the privileges of sons and daughters.

The implication of this is plain. Before Jesus came, men were not true children of God. At best they were immature children. Often they were disobedient and rebellious children. When God looked upon them, He saw they were far from His intention and desire.

And so, "when the fulness of the time was come," when the need was sorest, or, as the New English Bible suggests, when the work of preparation was complete, "God sent forth his Son" (Galatians 4:4), with the offer of pardon and restoration.

The greatest of our Lord's word-pictures of God is the

Parable of the Prodigal Son, but even that exquisite gem could not portray the whole truth. The fact is, the whole truth could not be told in words. It had to be set forth in a life, for the truth was not simply that, as in the peerless story, the Father waited and watched for His son's return and, when he appeared on the horizon, ran to welcome him. The truth was that the Father sent His firstborn Son to seek out the wanderer and bring him home.

That is the wonder of it. God's Son became a human Child. He was small, weak and helpless. He became a Man. He was subject to pain, disappointment, frustration, and sorrow. He was hedged about with limitations. "He laid His glory by." Is not this what perfect Love would do, thus to send, and to be willing thus to come?

He came to open the door into the fellowship of the Father's family, "that we might receive the adoption of sons" (Galatians 4:5). That was His desire for those among whom He lived. He wanted them to know "My Father and your Father" (John 20:17). That was the purpose of it all. To get ready for Christmas, our minds must be saturated with the tremendous thought that Jesus was born so that we might become "heirs of God, and joint-heirs with Christ" (Romans 8:17).

The purpose of the birth of Jesus is our complete reinstatement in the family of God. To prepare ourselves for Christmas, we must ponder the implications of this.

In 1533, on Advent Sunday, Dr. Martin Luther preached a sermon in which he said, "He leaves to other kings such things as pomp, castles, gold and wealth . . . but the craft which Christ the poor beggar-King knows, they do not know. He helps not against *my* sin only, but against *the whole world's sin.* He comes to take away not sickness only, but death; and not *my* death only, but *the whole world's death.*"

"This is a faithful saying, and worthy of all acceptation, that Christ Jesus came into the world to save sinners" (1 Timothy

1:15). "For this purpose the Son of God was manifested, that he might destroy the works of the devil (1 John 3:8). The Incarnation was the full and perfect revelation of God who, in offering Himself to the world, offered the world salvation. "Neither is there salvation in any other: for there is none other name under heaven given among men, whereby we must be saved" (Acts 4:12).

For God has other Words for other worlds,
But for this world the Word of God is Christ.
—Mrs. Hamilton King

We may question the first of these two lines, but there is no doubt about the second. "For this world, the Word of God *is* Christ." The Manger was the beginning, and the Ascension was the end of God's earthly redemptive revelation in Jesus. It was one revelation. It was the revelation of Emmanuel. He came to "save his people from their sins" (Matthew 1:21).

Some people would like to keep Jesus in the cradle. They do not want Him to grow up. Other people seem to want to keep Jesus on the Cross. They overlook the fact that His sojourn there was even briefer than His stay in the Manger. They forget, too, that the Cross in which Paul gloried (Galatians 6:14) was an *empty* Cross. Both these attitudes are wrong.

If we are to get ready for Christmas, we must bring ourselves to see that the whole emphasis of religion must not be laid on one aspect of it. We must accept the whole Christ. We must relate Christmas to the whole Christian Revelation. The Word became flesh for thirty-three hectic years, not for a few star-lit hours bathed in angelic splendor, nor for a few sickening hours shrouded in somber darkness.

To get ready for Christmas, we must grasp one thing on which the Gospels lay great stress. There is no blessing for us at the Cradle of Christ if we are unwilling to share His life of service, His agony in Gethsemane, His death at the hideous Place of a Skull, and His triumphant Resurrection on the glorious Hallelujah morn. Christ came to redeem the world. It is only as we give ourselves into His redemptive service that we can prepare our hearts for Christmas.

God, burst some star again, and let it blaze
In splendor that shall make the heavens grow dim;
That men from garish lights may lift their gaze
In wide-eyed wonder, and be led to Him.
O fill the sky with soft, glad wings once more,
To waft away men's grisly death-filled dew;
The heavenly music lost again restore;
O charm the earth afresh and make it new.
The tide of life has ebbed. Its foamy lace
Is far-horizoned now, and joys decay.
O let it flood anew each Christian place,
And even the atheist lands be drenched with spray.
This Christmas Day let heaven submerge the earth,
And all men know Thy Son has come to birth.

—James MacKay

1

Sing a Song of Bethlehem

O sing a song of Bethlehem,
Of shepherds watching there,
And of the news that came to them,
From angels in the air.

—Louis F. Benson

SING A SONG OF BETHLEHEM! BUT WHAT SONG SHALL WE sing? What canticle shall we choose to set forth our joyous praise? What glowing words shall enshrine our thoughts of Bethlehem?

Shall we make melody with the stately hymns which have enriched many a Christmas past? Shall we borrow the rollicking choruses of Germany, or the haunting cadences of France? Shall we echo the Latin chants of Gregorian grandeur with which the rafters of the monasteries rang long ago? Shall we turn to the New World for the new rhymes and the new rhythms which, born within living memory, add their graces to an ever-increasing hymnody? Shall we look to folk-tales for our expression, and discover in their artless creations the very art we seek? Shall the song we sing of Bethlehem find its consummation in a Babe in a manger, or in a partridge in a pear-tree?

Sing a song of Bethlehem! But they are so many, and they are so varied, we hardly know what to sing.

* * * * *

Each Advent, my family and I receive a beautiful assortment of Christmas cards. Their variety increases annually. Each year they seem more artistic, more aesthetic, more appealing — and more expensive.

We have acquired a marvelous diversity of pictures. There are lovely snow scenes which make us all the more thankful we live in sunny Florida! There is a magnificent painting of frigates running before a fair wind with every inch of canvas spread. The great clouds of pearl that hang forever upon the horizon of the sea bring back many precious memories of the Isles of June. One day I hope to frame this picture and hang it in my study.

There are plenty of illustrations of robins, holly, and ballet-dancers. There are little blond girls with expressions so angelic you know they exist nowhere but in the artists' minds.

There are charming vistas of sapphire lakes, and white-capped mountains, illuminated by the flamingo-colored haze of dawn. There are pathetic little wooden churches set among naked trees, under the grey sky of winter. There are ladies in hoop-skirts curtsying to gentlemen in stove-pipe hats. There is a Santa Claus with such a terrific beard he must be a bachelor, because only a child who wanted something very badly would kiss him!

One of my former teachers, that great scholar-preacher Dr. Norman G. Dunning, sent us a photograph of a famous fireplace, carved hundreds of years ago, of solid Italian mahogany.

It embellishes one of the great rooms in Haworth Hall, the historic mansion which is his home when he is in England.

Every time we have attacked a fresh batch of mail, I have had butterflies at the pit of my stomach. However, I am very relieved that we have come through another Christmas season without receiving Christmas cards with satellites on them!

Most of the traditional scenes have been improved. The reproductions of the Old Masters are skilfully done. Some of the stained-glass-window effects are so realistic I touched them with the tip of my finger to see what they are made of.

The wood-carvings of Africa, with their Black Christ, and the simple line-drawings of the Huron Indians, with a North American Christ in a New World wigwam, take their place beside Raphael's "Holy Family of the Oak Tree" and Rembrandt's "Virgin and Child."

* * * * *

You may be wondering what some of the carols I mentioned have to do with Christmas. You may, perhaps, have been puzzled to decide where "Winter Wonderland" and "Rudolph the Red-Nosed Reindeer" fit into the story.

You may be even more perplexed by some of the Christmas cards I have described. If we did not know the meaning of Christmas, many of the cards we receive would not give us much of a clue, would they? The only connection I can discover between Dr. Dunning's Italian fire-place card and Christmas is the remote possibility that Santa Claus might express his delight in its delicate craftsmanship by adding something extra to the stockings he finds hanging from it!

Yet if these folk-songs scatter a little happiness, and if these modern pictures awaken in our hearts the right response to something truly beautiful, I would be the last to play old Scrooge and go around muttering, "Humbug!"

Life's sweetest joys are hidden
In unsubstantial things;
An April rain, a fragrance,
A vision of blue wings.

—May Riley

The Elect enjoy Beauty for its own sake. There is, of course, more to it than that. What is mightiest always lies below the surface. Paul assured his converts, "All things are yours, for ye are Christ's, and Christ is God's" (1 Corinthians 3:23).

If we serve Him by whom and for whom "all things have been created" (Colossians 1:16), then we can surely adore Him with every facet of life, and with all the works of His hands. Calvin frequently insisted that the world is the theater of God's glory — *theatrum gloriae Dei,* as he called it. God is so great that all things give Him glory if we mean they should.

There is an intellectual climate in which religion is starved of the oxygen and sunshine it needs. There is an acid soil in which neither wonder, love, nor praise can take root. There is a dull, unimaginative temper in which such awesome truths as "The Word became flesh, and dwelt among us" (John 1:14), and "God so loved the world that he gave his only begotten Son" (John 3:16), can survive only as by a miracle.

I have mentioned Dickens' Scrooge. We need reminding of Ebenezer Scrooge at Christmas. He was a good man once. It was a single failing that got him down. He had enough spiritual energy to be faithful but not enough to be grateful.

There are many people like that. Their lives are enmeshed in serious solemnities. If they come to visit with you, they can stay longer in one hour than others in a whole week. They work so hard to "do the right thing" they never manage to "show the right spirit." They incline to the laws of Sparta rather than to the graces of Athens. Christmas shopping, when children stop, look, and glisten, frustrates them. They don't know what to do with Christmas. They grow uncomfortable as it approaches, like a teller expecting a visit from the bank examiner. They are afraid to rejoice, because they have not learned that we find God best in thanksgiving.

Saints who have mortified themselves to the quick are to be met with in every congregation of sincere worshipers. But how few who have enjoyed themselves to the utmost! How few elevated enough to believe that such joy would be acceptable to God!

Christmas comes to invite all of us to join again the merry, mystic circle of childhood. That is the way our Salvation lies. We shall not go far wrong if we gaily seek the child-heart. Without it no man shall see the Kingdom of God (Matthew 18:3). The tragedy of Christmas is not that we go upstairs to the nursery, but that we come down again.

* * * * *

In the barn at Bethlehem we see the Perfect Child. There He was, for the time, the youngest, the weakest, the poorest of them all. He was born in a barn to show what God thinks of human pride, of human ambition, of human loftiness, of human hardness. He was born in a barn to show what God thinks of those who turn to religion only because of what it can do for them. He was born in a barn to show what God thinks of those who always insist on having a place at the high table, and are miserable when others are put before them. He was born in a barn to show what God thinks of those personal jealousies and those family feuds that mar the fellowship God intended. Thank goodness something of this intention gets through to us at Christmas time.

Our hearts tonight are open wide,
The grudge, the grief, are laid aside.
The path and porch are swept of snow,
The door unlatched; the hearthstones glow —
No visitor can be denied.

All tender human homes must hide
Some wistfulness beneath their pride;
Compassionate and humble glow
Our hearts tonight.

Let empty chair and cup abide!
Who knows? Some well-remember stride
May come as once so long ago —
Then welcome, be it friend or foe!
There is no anger can divide
Our hearts tonight.[1]

The Babe was born in a barn to show how God despises the falsity of self-esteem, and the hypocrisy of flattery. The Babe was born in a barn to show how seldom appearance corresponds with reality.

* * * * *

The Babe was born in a barn to show how seldom appearance corresponds with reality.

A mother and her little girl were in a California department store, when a jolly-looking Santa Claus walked through. The child was thrilled. As he came near she said "Hello" brightly. "I'm not on till eleven o'clock," Santa replied dourly.

Was anything ever more incongruous than the birth of the Son of the Highest in the low squalid ugliness of the barn? Was anything ever less harmonious than the total situation which we call "Christmas"? It was a maze of contrasts and contradictions.

There was the lovely, blessed, and rejoicing Mother. Yet was ever a woman more alone and more care-burdened? There was the Holy Child bringing unsearchable wealth to men. Yet the men He came to enrich had no room for Him. There was

[1] "Christmas Eve," by Christopher Morley. From *Chimney Smoke,* published by J. B. Lippincott Co., copyright.

the greatness of His mission. There was the meanness of His birthplace.

There were the coarse, earthy shepherds under the silent stars. There was the angel-choir breaking that silence with the most exquisite minstrelsy of heaven. The men were shaken by the wonders they heard, and, like the animals, they huddled close.

There was the wretched and merciless Herod, growing in cruelty as he grew nearer death. There was the gentle Infant who came with peace and goodwill to men.

There were the fabulous Wise Men, pilgrims from the distant East, in search of light and hope. There were the chief priests and scribes of the people who were blind to what was happening on their own doorstep.

In it all, around it all, and through it all, in angel and dream, in event and word, in star and sign, in time and space, there was the presence of the Eternal God.

Wisemen in tracing Nature's laws
Ascend unto the highest cause,
Shepherds with humble fearfulness,
Walk safely, though their light be less;
Though Wisemen better know the way,
It seems no honest heart can stray.
There's no merit in the wise
But love (the shepherds' sacrifice).
Wisemen, all ways of knowledge past,
To th' shepherds' wonder come at last.

—Sidney Godolphin

The idyll of Bethlehem owes its transcendent beauty to its opposites, its contrasts, its contradictions, and its scope.

We must never forget its *scope.* Its appeal is universal because its scope is universal too. Everyone can "Sing a Song of Bethlehem" because its message is "to all people" (Luke 2:10).

Luke opens up to us the vistas of the ancient world. He paints a massive canvas. High in the background we see the grandeur that was Rome, with the haughty Caesar Augustus issuing the decree for all the world to be enrolled. Nearer at hand is the province of Syria, with Cyrenius in charge, temporarily at least. We see Palestine seething with the turmoil which marshals the Jews into their tribes and families, and herds them to their ancestral home. In the center foreground is the humble cave, the barn in which the Saviour found His first earthly rest. Bethlehem is there, thronged with an unfamiliar crowd. Its single street is busy, and every room is full. The picture is almost complete when, alongside the city, in the left foreground, there is sketched the hillside pastures where shepherds watch their flock by night, till suddenly the light of the moon and stars in the clear Syrian sky is dimmed by the unearthly brightness of a heavenly vision, revealing to them the wonders of Messiah's birth. Finally, the whole picture is framed and irradiated with an angelic host, and we are thrilled with its song of praise to God and peace to man.

* * * * *

The Christmas tidings were never more critically timely than they are today, when humanity appears to shiver on the brink of collective suicide. Although the *Pax Atomica* seems to offer a degree of security, men's hearts are shadowed by grim questionings.

Our age ought to study Luke's tableau. This weary, puzzled, and distracted twentieth century needs what Christmas has to give. Appalling cruelties, which mock the very essence of Christmas, claim that theirs is the way to prosperity, to order, and even to peace. Yet down into the midst of them descends this power in tenderness, this fearless, innocent, and noiseless Love.

How silently, how silently, the wondrous gift is given.

It will outlast noise and show, pomp and force, not because it is *of* God, but because it is *God Himself.*

Other festivals speak to us of what the Lord *has done.* Christmas speaks to us of what *He is.*

"They shall call his name Emmanuel; which is, being interpreted, God with us" (Matthew 1:23). This is the whole Gospel. This is the Christian Faith in a nutshell. Philosophy seeks Truth. The Gospel enshrines it.

"God with us." Here, in three short words, is the mighty message of Redemption. This is why Jesus was born into the world. This is why we should "Sing a Song of Bethlehem." The words are, of course, important, but of supreme importance is the spirit in our hearts.

"God with us." Why? As we enter into the joy of the Holy Child's birth, we must remember that He came to "save his people from their sins" (Matthew 1:21).

O Fire of our renewing Light
Which and by which we only see,
Let us not flee Thy burning, nor
Droop lids to shut out Thee:
Proud-bowed Prometheus never snatched such brands
As gently tender now God's tiny hands —
Behold them, burnt through, bone-bored, snapping, severing thy bands.

—S. L. Bethel

Our faith must never degenerate into stark sentimentality. Emotion has its place in our approach to Christmas. We must beware lest it should evaporate without having moved our hearts to faith and our wills to action. Nothing does us good unless it makes us good. Nothing makes us good unless it makes us good for something. In His sight we may be sheep, but He nowhere says we have to be sheeplike in our acceptance of conditions as we find them. Christmas does not speak to us unless it makes us so dissatisfied that we become crusaders.

Religion does not end in *feeling*. Neither does it feed upon sensation. If our emotion ends merely in stimulated feelings, we need to check up on ourselves. To be "filled with the Spirit" (Ephesians 5:18) is not to "feel good." It is to be in partnership with God. The Song of Bethlehem which we must sing is,

O Come, let us adore Him, Christ the Lord.

But here, as indeed everywhere else, we must sing "praises with understanding." To *adore* is to yield ourselves in glad response to the adorable. It is to lose ourselves in the love and service of Him whom we adore. We do not adore Him if we are not "laborers together with God" (1 Corinthians 3:9; cf. 2 Corinthians 6:1). Faith without works is not adoration. It is not even faith.

Christmas calls us to assume the responsibilities of discipleship. In it God urges His Church, the Body of Christ here on earth, to fulfill the task for which He created it, and take the message of His redeeming love to the ends of the world. Then, and only then,

Time will run back and fetch the Age of gold,
And speckled vanity
Will sicken soon and die,
And leprous Sin will melt from earthly mould;
And Hell itself will pass away,
And leave her dolorous mansions to the peering day.

Yea, Truth and Justice then
Will down return to men,
Orbed in a rainbow; and, like glories wearing,

Sing a Song of Bethlehem

Mercy will sit between
Throned in celestial sheen,
With radiant feet the tissued clouds down steering;
And Heaven, as at some festival,
Will open wide the gates of her high palace-hall.

—John Milton

2

The Miracle of Christmas

She brought forth her firstborn son . . .
and laid him in a manger (Luke 2:7).

IF "GOD WAS IN CHRIST" IN THAT MANGER; IF DIVINITY took human form in that manger; if "the Word became flesh" in that manger; there is only one possible explanation: "This is the Lord's doing, and it is marvelous in our eyes" (Psalm 118:23).

It was a *miracle*. Because it was a miracle, it is a *mystery*. It is nothing short of blasphemy to assume we have all the answers about the Almighty. I have little patience, I must confess, with those naïve souls who are quite confident they can always mark His ways, chart His course, and explain His acts.

We think of God, we think of the mystery of the Universe, but we do not think about it very much. We do not really believe it is a mystery, or that we could not understand it if it were explained to us. Perhaps that is because, when all is said and done, we do not really believe in God. In our hearts, we are convinced that it is our world, not His.

Whatever else God is, He must be unconditioned Majesty. His very Being must be beyond our highest thought. He must be unfettered. He must be unmoved, undefined, unexplained. The worst news possible would be the news that all we know is all there is. Lecerf, the Reformed theologian, once wrote, "The presence of mystery is the footprint of the Divine." Some part of every question remains unanswered. Elusiveness touches everything worthwhile.

If Christ was God from the beginning, we need not be surprised that the beginning was so wonderful: "Conceived by the Holy Ghost; born of the Virgin Mary."

How? I do not know. I cannot explain the birth of Jesus. But I fail to see why that should be a stumbling-block. I cannot explain His Resurrection or Ascension either. Both the beginning and the end of our Lord's earthly life are beyond finite understanding. Anyone who claims to "understand" Jesus Himself, does not know the first thing about Him. "Non-miraculous Christianity" is Christianity emptied of its most distinctive contents. Many of us, unfortunately, have no taste for the powers which are invisible. And yet, "the things which are seen are temporal; but the things which are not seen are eternal" (2 Corinthians 4:18).

At the Christmas season, our hearts are uplifted. Are they not filled with a joy and wonder which also pass our understanding? Can you explain the whole content of what you call "the Christmas spirit"? I can't — but that does not stop me from enjoying it.

Only something very special, something "out of this world" can account for the experience which is ours as we hear the old, old story of the Birth of the Holy Child.

That blessed mood,
In which the burthen of the mystery,
In which the heavy and weary weight
Of all this unintelligible world,
Is lightened.

—Wordsworth

There were moments in Old Testament history when the Prophets knew God was very near. They wanted to run away from Him, to hide from Him. They took off their shoes because they discovered they were standing on holy ground.

Each year, as we come with wonder and adoration to the matchless story of the Nativity, something like that happens to us. Like the flash of a fish in a stream, the Dayspring from on high lifts up our hearts. It is a blessed season. We rejoice again in the supreme act of God. It is a *miracle*. Because it is a miracle, it is a *mystery*.

* * * * *

What did the miracle of Christ's coming involve?

When we ask Paul, he tells us the Son of God exchanged the wealth of heaven for the poverty of earth (2 Corinthians 8:9).

No-one knows what heaven is really like. The descriptions men have presumed to give vary from the weird to the ridiculous. Every part of Scripture needs to be read in the spirit in which it was written. Literal answers to questions about life after death are mostly foolishness. In the Book of the Revelation, even John could write only in symbols, and no one has ever been able to find an interpretation of those symbols acceptable to all.

I like the story of the little girl who attended her first funeral. She was greatly impressed. The next day she informed the class of her experience. The teacher asked her if she had learned anything. She replied, "Yes, I learned what heaven is." "Do tell us," said the teacher. "Heaven," said the child very deliberately, "is where we rest from our *neighbors!*"

Now and then the skeptic pokes fun by asking Christians whether they will not get tired of playing harps in heaven after the first ten thousand years. He does not understand Christianity, but he does understand futility.

We all want to know what heaven is like. This is a perfectly natural longing. If we hope to go somewhere, we like to know what kind of a place it is before we arrive. Each of us pictures heaven for himself.

Olive Schreiner, in her *Dreams*, takes us to a mountain in heaven. On the summit a great man is working. He has come from the lowest depths of pain to the high places of delight.

> *And I saw the figure bend over its work,*
> *And the light from its face fell upon it.*
> *And I said to God, "What is it making?"*
> *And God said, "Music".*
> *And He touched my ears and I heard it;*
> *And after a long while I whispered*
> *To God, "This is Heaven".*

Sir Robert Baden-Powell, the founder of the world Boy Scout movement, has a little marker above his last resting-place showing his name, the dates of his birth and death, and underneath it the Scout sign — a circle with a dot in the center, — which means "Gone home." That is the authentic Christian insight.

Do we know this earth? Do we know the volcanic mountains and the fearful earthquakes which wipe out peaceful communities? Do we know the vast oceans, the cruel storms, the grim icebergs, and the treacherous currents, which sink noble ships and devastate splendid shores? Do we know the tragic mine disasters, the barren Sahara, the swirling dust-bowls, and the slimy Renos, Monte Carlos, Harlems, and Skid Rows?

Yes, we know our world and the people in it. We know the glory and the grandeur, the fear and the hopelessness, the hate and the strife, the greed and the guilt. Who in his senses would exchange heaven for earth? Yet Paul insists this is precisely what the Son of God did!

* * * * *

Our Lord was of heavenly origin. There has never been anyone like Him. He is unique. There is in Him an immensity, a height, a depth, which no other life has revealed in all history. The Son of Mary — and the Son of God. He lived His life in the sunshine of God's smile. The hilltops and the stars kept His secret.

As a *Teacher,* He is profound, yet simple. He is so profound that we of this twentieth century have not exhausted the content of what He uttered in the first. His language is so simple "the common people heard him gladly" (Mark 12:37). "Never man spake like this man" (John 7:46).

In *prayer,* He is conscious not only that God is His Father, but also that He is the Christ, the pre-existent, eternal Son of God. "And now, O Father, glorify thou me with thine own self with the glory which I had with thee before the world was" (John 17:5).

The *claims* He makes concerning Himself could not be made by anyone else. They would be outrageous on any other lips. "I am the bread of life" (John 6:35). "I am the light of the world" (John 8:12). "Before Abraham was, I am" (John 8:58). "I am the good shepherd" (John 10:11, 14). "I am the resurrection and the life" (John 11:25). "I am the true vine" (John 15:1). "I and my Father are one" (John 10:30).

His *promises* are unique. "Come unto me, and I will give you rest" (Matthew 11:28). "Him that cometh to me I will in no wise cast out" (John 6:37). "I will make you fishers of men" (Mark 1:17). "Whosoever shall confess me before men, him will I confess before my Father which is in heaven" (Matthew 10:32). "I will not leave you orphans, I will come to you" (John 14:18).

He declares that He is the One about whom all the Prophets have spoken (Luke 24:27). He takes the attitude of God towards men (Luke 15:1, 7; Mark 5:34; Matthew 9:36; etc.). The Person of Jesus is central to the Gospel.

* * * * *

The Person of Jesus is central to the Gospel because if you take it away you have no Gospel left.

The Gospel is based on *who Jesus is,* as well as on *what He did.* Indeed, what He did depends on who He is.

When we say, "God was in Christ" (2 Corinthians 5:19), or, He is "the only begotten of the Father" (John 1:14), or, Jesus is "the Son of God" (Galatians 2:20), we mean He was both God and Man.

Many learned men have written many learned books in an attempt to solve the enigma of this belief. They have tried to explain it so we can understand it. If you like, they have tried "to make sense of it." I have read many of their books and have been able to understand a few of them. I am not sure even the authors understand some of the others. When Robert Browning was once asked about an obscure stanza he had written years before, he replied, "When that was written, there were two who knew what it meant, Almighty God and Robert Browning. Now only God knows!" I am sometimes tempted to think that theologians imagine anything they don't understand must be profound. This is not necessarily the case. It may be unintelligible.

This is not to decry the efforts of man to know all he can about his Maker. But when we talk about the Person of Jesus Christ we are dealing with the supreme miracle of history, and when all is said and done, it is still the supreme mystery.

Jesus, the Son of Mary, was the Son of God. The fact remains. The explanations "vanish away," as Paul said they would (1 Corinthians 13:8).

The Son of God became the Son of Mary that first Christmas, in all the degradation of Bethlehem's cattle stall. There, He by whom and for whom "all things were created" (Colossians 1:16), "who is the image of the invisible God" (Colossians 1:15; cf. 2 Corinthians 4:4), "took upon him the form of a servant, and was found in fashion as a man" (Philippians 2:7f.).

Christ, by highest heaven adored,
Christ the everlasting Lord,
Late in time behold Him come,
Offspring of a virgin's womb!
Veiled in flesh the Godhead see;
Hail the Incarnate Deity.

What began at Bethlehem continued on earth for thirty-three years. No one ever came to Him in vain. Lepers of repulsive appearance knelt to Him. They were cured by a touch or a word (Mark 1:40f.; Luke 17:12ff.; etc.). He healed the blind (Matthew 9:27ff.; Mark 8:22ff.; 10:46ff.; Luke 7:21; John 9:1ff.; etc.); the lame (Matthew 11:5; John 5:2ff.; etc.); the deaf and dumb (Mark 7:32ff.; 9:17ff.; etc.). He raised the dead (Matthew 9:18ff.; Luke 7:12ff.; John 11:43f.).

Jesus always spoke to men as if they were capable of receiving truth and as if they were even interested in it. He told wicked people their sins were forgiven. The scribes and Pharisees balked at that. For once they put their finger on the heart of the problem, "Who can forgive sins, but God alone?" (Luke 5:21). There is only one possible answer — No one!

Jesus did all these things the New Testament records of Him

because He was not only the Son of Mary, but the Son of God also.

In her famous play *The Man Born to Be King,* Dorothy L. Sayers makes one of the Wise Men say, "I speak for the sorrowful people. We rise up to labor, and lie down to sleep, and the night is only a pause between one burden and another. Fear is our daily companion, fear of want, the fear of war, the fear of cruel death, and of still more cruel life. . . . But all this we could bear if we knew that we did not suffer in vain; that God was beside us in the struggle, sharing the miseries of His own world. For the riddle that torments the world is this, Shall sorrow and Love be reconciled at last?"

Christmas is the answer to that. The message of Advent is that God is beside us in the struggles and miseries of our world, because it is His world too. In Jesus, God became flesh of our flesh. Love and sorrow met and were reconciled. God *is* "with us,"

Pleased as man with men to dwell,
Jesus, our Immanuel.
—Charles Wesley.

* * * * *

The Wise Men asked, "Where is he that is born King of the Jews?" (Matthew 2:2). When Jesus was crucified, a notice was nailed to the Cross, "Jesus of Nazareth, the King of the Jews" (John 19:19).

When we look at Him, we do not find a single characteristic of royalty. He lacks everything of which earthly monarchs boast. Yet we firmly believe in the kingship of Christ. It is a kingship unaccompanied by the outward trappings of power. He has none of these because He needs none. He is King in Himself.

He is not King because of what He *has.* He is not King even because of what He *does.* He is King because of what He *is.*

He reigns in Love. He forces Himself upon none. He offers Himself to all. He does not rely on raw might, but on Truth and on its ability to win our free and glad consent. He seeks not slaves, but friends (John 15:15).

Jesus came to bear witness to the Truth. He tells Pilate, "To this end was I born, and for this cause came I into the world" (John 18:37). The Babe in the Manger is the Truth of God. He is the eternal Truth shaped, fashioned, and made human.

The expansion of the Christian Faith in the life of mankind is always to be tested by the standard of Truth which is Christ Himself. His claim to be the King of men, the Ruler of the Kingdom of Truth, is the basis of our belief that the Gospel is a universal Faith for all mankind. Our world is full of berserk creeds that try to make a nation, or race, or social group, divine. But Truth is Truth whether you are a Hindu or a Hottentot, a Russian or an American. The Kingdom of Truth is one. That is a self-evident proposition. Only those philosophies which claim to be universal have any right to be heard. Any philosophy of life or religion that makes its appeal only to one section of mankind is immediately brushed off as inadequate by thinking people.

Jesus reigns in Patience, too. He counts no rejection as final. He never gives in. He never casts off. He makes His way in the world not by majorities, but by martyrdoms. He turns defeat itself into an opportunity for victory more splendid than before.

His rule is invisible, but potent. The kingdoms of this world stand when they embrace something of His Spirit. They perish when they refuse to do this.

The King came that first Christmas, seeking our allegiance and loyalty. Nowadays our loyalty and allegiance is like that of the dying Irishman. The priest arrived at his home to give him extreme unction. He asked Pat to renounce the devil and all evil works. The dying man whispered, "Sure and begorrah, your reverence, but I'm hardly in a position to antagonize anyone"! We have made the Irishman's last word a national motto. We want to please everybody. The unpardonable sin of twentieth-century culture is to have principles and to stand for them. We need to hear again that great pronouncement of Dante, "The hottest places in hell are reserved for those who, in a period of moral crisis, maintain their neutrality."

The King came that first Christmas, and although His Sovereignty is in no way affected by our response, yet our co-operation, or lack of it, determines both the speed and the extent of His success. We talk about commitment, we sing about it, we even pray about it. We will gladly give up anything which we never really wanted to retain, but the fact is, we are not prepared for an absolutely complete and unconditional surrender of ourselves to Christ. Then we gripe about the meager success of the Church!

We want Peace. "Peace" is an anointed word. It is the grand passion of our age. Peace has become an obsession with us. We want Peace at any price. We cannot have Peace at any price. We are so haunted with one aspect of Peace — the absence of war — that our conception of it has become distorted. You cannot isolate one element in Peace and say, "That is Peace." It is not Peace. It may be one ingredient in Peace. It can be nothing more. Even then, it is a negative idea, and it is always a poor principle to build on a negative.

Just as you cannot isolate one element in Peace, so you cannot isolate Peace itself. It is not an end in itself. Like happiness, it is a by-product. Peace can never be divorced from Righteousness. That is why the Bible never separates them. When we have Righteousness, we shall not have to worry about Peace. "Peace on earth" is "among men with whom he is well pleased" (Luke 2:14). While the earth remains, there will never be a time when men will not be called upon to sacrifice themselves for Righteousness' sake. The Cross will not die out of human experience, nor need we fear that it will ever become an easy thing in this world to do right.

Peace? When have we prayed for peace?
Is there no wrong to right?
Wrong crying to God on high
Here where the weak and the helpless die,
And the homeless hordes of the city go by,
The ranks are rallied to-night!

Peace? When have we prayed for peace?
Are ye so dazed with words?
Earth, heaven shall pass away
Ere for your passionless peace we pray!
Are ye deaf to the trumpet that calls us to-day,
Blind to the blazing swords?

—Alfred Noyes

The scandal of the relaxed moral nerve penetrates every facet of our civilization. We want the benefits of the Kingdom without the rule of the King. When we crown Him King of our lives and behave like His subjects, the benefits of His Kingdom will follow. *Ubi Deus ibi pax.*

When we ask Him to reign over us, Jesus reveals Himself to us as King, though not to terrify us. He comes with a word of power matched to our need. He comes in all the radiance of His glory, but He does not come mechanically, with an automatic sameness. The divine response to human needs is as varied as the needs to which it responds.

This is the witness of the New Testament. It is confirmed by the testimony of multitudes of humble believers in every age and clime.

The mechanics of His coming to the individual are as obscure as the manner by which He came to Mary. It, too, is a Miracle. It is the work of the same God who clothed

Himself with human garb in Bethlehem long ago. *He who came to this world in Jesus has never left it.* He is its King.

Lo, within a manger lies
He who built the starry skies,
He who, throned in height sublime,
Sits amid the cherubim.

—Edward Caswall

Ah, Lord, who hast created all,
How hast Thou made Thee weak and small,
That Thou must choose Thy infant bed
Where ass and ox but lately fed?

—Martin Luther

* * * * *

Is it any wonder that mystery was added to mystery in this great Miracle? Is it any wonder that heavenly hosts lifted the music of the spheres into a sublime symphony of praise? Is it any wonder that Wise Men from the East left the comfort and security of their lavish homes, invested their wealth in costly presents, and followed a Star hung out like a lamp in the heavens?

Is it any wonder that on every anniversary of that blessed event we escape the limitations of earthbound prose, and express our holiest joy in the soaring language of the noblest poetry?

The majestic cadences of "*Adeste Fideles,*" and the other glorious carols we have sung since we were children, never weary us. They call up memories of "the dear dead days beyond recall." They stir our hearts, for their story is deathless. But they do more than that. The magic of Christmas past acts as midwife to Christmas present. "Unto you," said the angel, "is born a Saviour, Christ the Lord" (Luke 2:11).

With each passing year, with Christmas added to Christmas and memory heaped on memory, this becomes more and more personalized. The message is for us. He is born *for us*.

This is the Miracle of Christmas. It leads us to be *worshipers* at the manger. *Our hearts* go forth in adoration and gratitude, in wonder and praise, as did the hearts of the simple Shepherds and the Wise Men of old.

3

God's Unspeakable Gift

MARTIN LUTHER WROTE THIS ABOUT CHRISTMAS, "IT IS not simply an old story of an event that happened fifteen hundred years ago; it is more than an event that happened once; for it is a gift and a bestowing that endures for ever."

For us who read these wise words of the learned Reformer, the fifteen hundred years across which he looked back have lengthened out to nearly two thousand. But the additional four and a half centuries of Christian experience have only served to emphasize the truth he uttered. "It is a gift and a bestowing that endures for ever."

Paul says, "God loveth a cheerful giver" (2 Corinthians 9:7). What He admires in others, He is in Himself. At Christmas time, when

. . . the open hand
Scatters its bounty over sea and land,

we see Almighty God giving *Himself*. The birth of Jesus shows to us that amazing generosity in giving which is of the very essence of God's own nature. "Thanks be to God for his unspeakable gift" (2 Corinthians 9:15), is the theme-song of Christianity.

"Unspeakable" is a popular word with people whose vocabulary is limited and whose observation is superficial. As they see vaguely and inexactly, they readily resort to such resounding words as have no clear-cut picture in them. But Paul was not one of these. He not only peered into the essential nature of things, he also labored diligently to find the best word to express what he saw. When no such word existed, he did not hesitate to make up his own. If Paul calls the gift of God "unspeakable," it is not from looseness or from indolence. It is because he can neither find a word nor manufacture one that will do justice to his thought.

* * * * *

The word which the New Testament uses to describe the unspeakable generosity of God is "Grace." It is one of the master-words of our Faith.

"Grace" sums up all that is represented in the Old Testament by such fine phrases as "loving kindness" and "tender mercy." It adds a new dimension as well. It means more than the full, free and unmerited favor of God. It tells us *God took the initiative.* He came to meet our desperate human need. Grace is not an attractive sentiment. It is a redeeming energy embodied in a Redeeming Personality.

The word "condescension" retains its original meaning only when it is used of our Lord Jesus Christ. Of Him alone can it be said, "He condescended," "He came down," "He humbled Himself," "He became poor in becoming man." He was so Divine that angels sang over His coming, giving glory to God. He was so human that a lowly village maiden tucked Him into the hay.

The joyous Gospel of Christmas proclaims that Almighty God entered our human life in the most generous manner possible. He came in the way which would be the greatest help to those earthly ones who most needed His heavenly aid. He chose to lay His head on the pillow of poverty. He chose a cradle which was the crudest of all cradles. He chose a shelter which the beasts had used. What He began on a bed of common hay, He finished on the hard wood of the Cross.

When we ponder the Christmas story, faith is renewed, hope is restored, and love is reinforced. Here God commits Himself to man. Christmas is not a promise. It is a fulfillment. Here is a Baby. This Child is the Incarnate Word. This Word is Incarnate Love. "Thanks be to God for his unspeakable gift."

* * * * *

It is a great part of the wonder of Christmas that God should reveal Himself not only *to* man, but also *in* man. It is almost incredible

That He whom the sun serves, should faintly peep
Through clouds of infant flesh; that He, the old
Eternal Word should be a Child, and weep;
That He who made the fire should fear the cold;
That heaven's High Majesty His court should keep
In a clay cottage, by each blast controll'd.

In spite of our kinship with the beasts that perish, in spite of our folly, iniquity and shame, we are brethren of Him in Whom God is fully seen.

For Mercy has a human heart,
Pity a human face;
And Love, the human form divine,
And peace, the human dress.

When God came to take His share in that part of the world's history in which His human life was to be spent, He came clothed in the garment of frail human flesh.

His coming was unnoticed, unknown, and unrecognized. Here was the most wonderful of all happenings in time. Here the strong Son of God was born as the weak Son of Mary. Here was a new, all-appealing, all-revealing, and all-redeeming manifestation of Eternal God. Yet men did not recognize Him. They had neither time nor room for Him.

We talk sentimentally about there being no room for Him in the squalid inn of Bethlehem. What is far more important is that there is no room for Him in the inn of the human heart. There was no room for Him then. There is no room for Him now.

Yet even though He finds no room in the inn we call our heart, there is room for all of us in the Inn we call the heart of God. There is room in God's Inn for every temperament and every type, for every kindred, tribe, people, and tongue. God's unspeakable gift is *unto us!*

Unto us?
Lord, unto whom?
The fair-skinned, favored,
genteel few?
Just to them?
Or unto Jew,
Oriental, Negro,
Sioux?
Unto these?
Yes, unto all
the human family,
great and small.
Christ Child,
with your arms stretched wide,
forgive our prejudice,
and pride.

—Helen Earle Simcox

God's Unspeakable Gift

What we think about God affects all our thinking. All our thinking affects all our praying. All our praying affects all our lives.

If we think about God as One who has room in His great loving heart for the whole world, as One who wants the whole world to come to Him, it will make our entire thought-life more worthy. It will make our prayer-life more earnest. It will make our life of service more devoted — and more costly.

Jesus, and Paul after Him, taught self-denial for the sake of others. The ascetics taught self-denial for the sake of self. The world, to them, was not something to be saved, but something to be saved from. This heresy persists in unenlightened Protestant Pietism. When it says, "Thanks be to God for his unspeakable gift," it really means, "Thanks be to God for his unspeakable gift *to me*." Thus it tends to build pride and complacency. When we pray for understanding, we ask for insight into God's purpose for us, which must be part of His purpose for all His children. So we cannot accept "the gift of God" for ourselves unless we are eager to share it with others.

Not cloistered saints, that bid the world
Remember they forget — its lure defy,
Whose abnegating robes accost the glance
Of lost humanity;
Not they whose moving lips attest
Repeated prayer, to shame the throng or mart,
Whose fingers outward clasp a crucifix;
Not they who stand apart —
Are Thy swift followers alone,
Sweet Christ! Unveiled, untonsured, they there be
Who hold their mired brothers to their heart,
Even for love of Thee,
Who didst remember to the end

Thy world, though they had Thee forgot and fled —
A hillside Calvary Thy holy lot,
Mountain and sea Thy bed.

—Martha Gilbert Dickinson

* * * * *

Around the birth of Jesus, reverent devotion has gathered a wealth of color and romance, but the real miracle of Christmas is Jesus Himself. It is not the wonder of His birth. It is the wonder and glory of Him who was born.

For most of us, Christmas is the birthday of Jesus. It is right and proper that we should think of it in this way, so long as we do not stop there.

This is what I mean: The early Christians were quite sure *Christmas was not the beginning of Jesus.* Birth is usually regarded as the beginning, so they thought of Christmas as the birthday of the Gospel, rather than the birthday of Christ. It was, for them, the birthday of the Good News which was the great revealing of God "in human flesh appearing."

The New Testament says Jesus was with God from all eternity (John 1:1). The world was made by Him, and without Him was not anything made that was made (John 1:3; I Corinthians 8:6; Hebrews 1:2). He was, and is, the brightness of the Father's glory (Hebrews 1:3). He upholds all things by the word of His power (Colossians 1:17; Hebrews 1:3).

He was in the world long before that first Christmas. He was in the world, and the world knew Him not (John 1:10). He came to His own folks at Bethlehem (John 1:11), but "the husbandmen, when they saw the son, said among themselves, This is the heir; come, let us kill him, and take his inheritance. And they took him, and cast him forth out of the vineyard, and killed him" (Matthew 21:38f.). He is "the Lamb slain from the foundation of the world" (Revelation 13:18).

Here are some of the wonderful names and titles which the Bible and the Psalmody of Christendom ascribe to "Him who in a manger laid": Saviour, Redeemer, Pattern, Example, Hero, Leader, Captain, Strong Son of God, Master, Lord, Teacher, Prince of Glory, Shepherd, Priest, Guardian, Prophet, Rock, King, Deliverer, Salvation, Prince of Peace, Great David's Greater Son.

There are many others, but this list is adequate for the purpose. If we think about each of these designations, and then try to combine all the ideas they involve, we shall begin to catch a faint glimpse of what Jesus can be in the experience of those who fully trust Him. This is the Christ we must celebrate at Christmas.

The trouble is that for every thousand people who talk about getting ready for *Christmas,* there is only one who earnestly gets ready for *Christ*. If we do not prepare for Him, Christmas will come and go without giving us even a taste of the very special happiness which He always brings to those who are ready to welcome and receive Him.

The thing that really matters at Christmas is the thing that so often and so foolishly we forget — that this particular Baby whose birth we celebrate, this "Maker and Monarch and Saviour of all," was born to be *King*.

He was born to be King in England, where there is a Queen; in America, where there is a President; in Russia, where there is a Dictator. He was born to be King of everybody in the whole world. He was born to be King in your life and in mine.

When we realize this, we shall come to see that what He wants from us is not cradle-songs and lullabies, not only admiration, affection, and homage, but commitment, loyalty, and obedience.

Christmas today is something of a racket. Big business cashes in on sentimentality. Commercials are far more important than carols. The message of what *man* has to *sell* takes precedence over the proclamation of what *God* has to *give*. No wonder this kind of Christmas is here today and gone tomorrow. Like the house built on sand, it lacks foundations and gets carried away by the next tidal-wave of spending, usually the January sales.

Real Christmas is "something out of this world." It involves the recognition that something happened at Bethlehem more than nineteen hundred years ago that has completely changed our relationship with God.

He deigns in flesh to appear,
Widest extremes to join,
To bring our vileness near,
And make us all divine.

—Charles Wesley

It involves the recognition that what we could never do for ourselves, God has done for us in Christ. There are some things for which you cannot render formal thanks in formal words. When we begin to see something of what God has done for us in Christ, it evokes the heartfelt ejaculation, "Thanks be to God for his unspeakable gift."

* * * * *

The backdrop of miracle is provided by the heavenly light, the song of the angels, and the star guiding the pilgrims. It is all in keeping with the mighty proclamation of the New Testament and of the Church, that the Babe of Bethlehem was the eternal Lord of heaven, the only begotten Son of the Father.

So in our Christmas rejoicing we turn to poetry to express the wonder of The Good News, and through poetry we rise to the most sublime theology.

True God of true God;
Light of light eternal;
Lo! He abhors not the Virgin's womb.
Son of the Father,
Begotten, not created:
O come, let us adore Him,
Christ the Lord.

Anonymous, 17th or 18th Century,
translated by Frederick Oakeley

Perhaps for us who are too ready to dwell on the darkness of our times, the "Light of light eternal" speaks of the light which dawned in the wonder of that stable long ago, "the sunburst out of the East, flooding the world with day."

All our talk about Christmas, mixed up with H-bombs, rockets, and warring ideologies, must deepen our hopelessness unless we really believe that the Light will *never* be overcome by the darkness.

The Star was such a small light in that Syrian night sky. Yet it led some earnest seekers after truth to a very little Child, who turned out to be King of kings and Lord of lords. The Light of the world shines bright in Bethlehem.

If we think *we* need that Light, what about *them?* Palestine was an enemy-occupied country. Rome had an army of occupation there. You need to live in an enemy-occupied country to know what it is like: the hardship, the fear, the uneasiness, the brutality of the mercenaries, the injustice of the foreign overlords, the corruption of the imported officialdom, the greed of the tax-gatherers, the whip of the task-masters, the lust of the conquerors, the living death of the concentration camp.

In a very illuminating paragraph, the Beloved Physician tells us, "In the fifteenth year of the reign of Tiberias Caesar, Pontius Pilate being governor of Judaea, and Herod (being) Tetrarch of Galilee, and his brother Philip Tetrarch of Iturea, and Lysanias the Tetrarch of Abilene, Annas and Caiaphas being high priests, the word of God came . . ." (Luke 3:1ff.). If you wanted to start a Rogues' Gallery, it would be difficult to find a more repulsive lot of crooks with which to begin. To match them, you would have to go to the courts of Nero, Pope Alexander VI, Hitler, or Peron.

Jesus was born into a world of corruption and tyranny. We have become fairly hardened to atrocity stories in our time. They are nothing new. Herod's slaughter of the Innocents (Matthew 2:16ff.) and Pilate's massacre of the worshippers in the Temple (Luke 13:1) belong to the same category. Jesus came into a world very much like our own. It was a world of moral degradation. It was a world of national humiliation, low ethical standards, bitter hatred, and unrelieved despair.

Jesus lived in that kind of world. He did not dwell in some sort of Shangri-La, where birds were always singing in the azure sky. He lived in a hard world, a world of hungry children. Jesus lived under the watchful eye of coarse soldiers. He lived within earshot of spies and fifth-columnists.

Yet the coming of Jesus gave this troubled, needy, debauched world the opportunity of a fresh start. That is why men have renumbered the years from the date of His birth.

The world had grown old and tired and gray. People were walking about like zombies. They were lifeless and listless. They had no light in their eye. There was no spring of confidence in their step. They could not see any meaning or purpose in what they were doing. They did not know why they were living. God seemed far, far away.

Even earnest, thoughtful men and women had come to imagine they were left on their own, to do the best they could; but they knew their best was not very good. They were being defeated by what happened to them. They were being crushed by the sheer weight of adverse circumstances. They were tired of living. They were afraid to die.

Into such a world, right from the heart of God, came Jesus. He came to meet their every need. He came to *give*. He came to give to all who would receive Him life, power, energy, vision, the ability to get on top of circumstances, to be strong where they used to be weak, and to be brave where they used to be fearful. The Beloved Disciple says, "As many as received him, to them he gave the power to become sons of God" (John 1:12). That is the very thing *we* need right now.

"Power to become sons of God" means the ability to be the kind of people that in our best moments we want to be, but which, in spite of all our good resolutions and sincere efforts, we fail to be. Because Jesus came to give us this power, Christmas is a time when loyalties are made sturdy, when hope is born anew, when we rejoice because

> *Night's candles are burnt out, and jocund day*
> *Stands tip-toe on the misty mountain-tops.*
> —Shakespeare

We can afford to rejoice if we remember that God has visited and redeemed His people, and has raised up a mighty salvation for us (Luke 1:68f.).

When Oliver Cromwell lay dying, his friends gathered round his bed with long faces. The women started weeping. It was a scene of unrelieved sadness. Suddenly the grand old man raised himself on his elbow and growled, "Is there nobody here will praise God?" That is the authentic voice of Christian experience.

On March 5, 1945, Ernst von Harnack, civil servant and son of the most distinguished theologian of his day, was executed by Hitler's orders. When taken to prison, he discovered that the man in the adjacent cell had a violin. His great desire was to witness for his Lord and Master on the day of his death. Accordingly, he arranged with his neighbor that he should play an accompaniment when he was led out to die. The morning of his execution came. The cell door was flung open. A harsh command rapped out. As the condemned man stepped into the corridor there rang out from the next cell a song of triumph:

The Royal banners forward go,
The Cross shines forth in mystic glow,
Where He in flesh, our flesh who made,
Our sentence bore, our ransom paid.

Venantius Fortunatus, A.D. 530

The early Christians did not rejoice because of better things to come. They rejoiced because Christ had come. God's Unspeakable Gift was not provisional. They rejoiced because it was final. We are not afraid to face all the calamity, hatred, and tragedy of the world, because we have this confidence, *God has acted.*

To celebrate Christmas worthily, we must recognize that it is the time and place when we cease worrying about what the world is coming to, and rejoice greatly in what has come to the world. "Thanks be to God for his unspeakable gift."

* * * * *

The Christmas story has everything. Innocence, love and lore, simplicity, music and mystery, a Star, a song and a small Son — these elements are all here. If we are not too withered by the world's woes, they will bring a wealth of warmth and wonder to our hearts.

Christmas Day is the dearest and most delightful day of the year, because it is the greatest and gentlest gesture of God's generosity. "Unto us a Son is given" (Isaiah 9:6). No cold calculating of this or that mars the exquisite simplicity of the Divine Grace.

God's gift is outright. It is unutterable, unspeakable. It is "given, not lent" and "not withdrawn once sent." It is for Christmas Day and for every day. It is for every day because we need it every day. Our emptiness invites God's abundance. Our weakness cries out for His strength. Our blindness gropes for His guiding hand.

When we gather in reverent adoration around the Son of God in the straw-lined crib, the Still Small Voice speaks the strengthening word that sin will never be allowed to gain the final victory, that the fire He came to kindle will never be put out.

But let us get our perspective right. In the light of the setting sun even the smallest objects throw long shadows. Let us give first place to first things. As we approach the Holy Night, let us examine our priorities.

Let us come to Christmas this year with this thought burnt into our minds:

The most important questions of our day is not,
When will we reach the moon?
The most important question of our day is,
When will we go to Bethlehem?

4

The Babe and the Bully

CHRISTMAS IS A VERY PRECIOUS SEASON TO ALL CHRISTIAN people. Whether we are young or old as we measure time, we find we can be young in spirit at this period of the year.

When we hear again the majestic words of the Advent story, words which have lost none of their grandeur through familiarity, it is as though we are transported into another world, where everything is pure and true, lovely and of good report. Hope radiates from the Gospel.

Whatever else Christmas may have done, it has set the Church to singing. It supplies the three factors which Bernard Manning found in the great hymns of Charles Wesley: "The solid structure of historic dogma, the passionate thrill of present experience, the glory of a mystic sunlight coming directly from another world." When we sing the glorious carols, we approach the heart of our religion. We drink of the brook by the way. There never was such gaiety as this. I have heard some congregational singing which sounded strangely like an angry crowd howling for blood. But not at the season of the Holy Nativity. Its music is pitched in the key of rejoicing.

Christians, awake, salute the happy morn,
Whereon the Saviour of the world was born.

—John Byrom

All my heart this night rejoices.

—Paulus Gerhardt

Happy all who hear the message
Of His coming from above.

—George Stringer Rowe

And therefore be merry, set sorrow aside;
Christ Jesus our Saviour was born on this tide.

—Traditional

Good Christian men rejoice
With heart and soul and voice.

—John Mason Neale

God rest you merry, gentlemen,
Let nothing you dismay.

—Traditional

In the sheer ecstasy of the hour, we forget that within a very short time the parents, with their Firstborn, had to gather everything together in the middle of the night, to take a hurried journey into a foreign country, in terrified flight from the hired killers of the mad King Herod. We often fail to distinguish the clatter of their iron-soled sandals on Bethlehem's cobbled street.

* * * * *

The shock which came to Herod when he heard of a "*born* king of the Jews" (Matthew 2:2) was so great that he momentarily lost his aplomb. He blurted out the first thing that came into his mind, "Go and search diligently for the young child; and when ye have found him, bring me word again, that I may come and worship him also" (Matthew 2:8). He could have bitten off his tongue as soon as the words were out of his mouth. They were obviously ridiculous. He could not recognize a new king without abdicating his own position, and everyone knew he would never do that.

He did some fast talking, and some faster thinking. He seized on the fact that Abraham was his ancestor. He emphasized that he belonged to the elder branch of Isaac's race. He professed devout interest in the fulfillment of the promise to his family. He pictured it as the consummation of all his hopes and prayers. He was a suave talker, and, if he did not hoodwink the Wise Men, he deceived himself into thinking he had done so. He was probably gleeful when they left the palace. His gloom on hearing of a possible rival was dissipated by the ease with which he thought his nimble mind had outwitted the learned sages. He confidently looked for their return.

The days passed. At last it became apparent to Herod that the Magi were not going to come back and give him the information he desired. His subsequent rage knew no bounds.

They had dealt him a double affront. Not only had they made a mockery of his regal authority by flouting his request, they had added insult to injury by out-foxing him. The Wise Men had detected the goat's foot in Herod. He could not bear that, for he was particularly sensitive on this point. He could never escape the fact of his Idumean origin. He knew what this meant to the people he ruled. He could take no pride in his ancestry with them, no matter what kind of front he tried to put up before strangers.

His vanity, therefore, was centered in himself and in his extraordinary political acumen. Everything he possessed he had gained by his wits. The fact that he was consistently successful in dealing with people made him all the more vulnerable on those remarkably few occasions when he was too smart for his own good.

Herod had built a magnificent Temple to the God of the Jews. He had erected several lesser temples on Jewish soil to the hated gods of the Gentiles. He had no religion of his own. He worshipped only himself. His hasty statement to the Wise Men was about as sincere as an undertaker's get-well card. He did not care that it was merely a subterfuge, but he cared very much that it had been recognized as such.

When he discovered that his trick had backfired, his first thought was probably to avenge himself upon the Magi, but they were over the hills and far away by that time. Maddened by such anger as only a frustrated despot can know, Herod resolved on far more desperate measures than he had first intended. Instead of destroying one Child whose existence was a threat to the continuation of his house, he determined to murder "all the male children that were in Bethlehem, and in all the borders thereof, from two years old and under" (Matthew 2:16).

Herod was the first of a long line of rulers who have feared the rival claims of the Babe. Until the evil Hitler knew his strength, he proceeded cautiously. He could not be sure how the Babe, represented by His Church, would react to his claims. Politeness was necessary until the issue became clear.

In modern Russia the skein of Church-State relations is tangled. Initial persecution has been followed by tolerance. But what will be the end of the story? Herod is obviously troubled, and at the moment seems to be polite. The Church is tolerated, at a price. The situation is uneasy. Herod knows the rival claims of the Babe; should they ever seem to threaten his personal interests, his mood might be very different.

In any part of the world where the State has claimed for itself the allegiance which really belongs to God, it nervously hears of the Babe. The fact that Castro made his initial attacks on the Church at the Advent season is significant. So also is the length of time which elapsed before he "requisitioned" her schools.

In the West, as in the East, totalitarian states will not welcome a rival claim to obedience. For a time they may practice caution. They may even manifest a polite toleration. But it is an uneasy truce. It is wholly dependent upon what effect Bethlehem and its manger have upon Jerusalem and the palace of the king.

This strange discord jars the sweet music of Christmas. Perhaps that is why we usually ignore it, or why some people have tried to explain it away. Their efforts have not been too successful. It is absurd to compare the story of the Flight into Egypt as the New Testament parallel of the Old Testament record of the sojourn of the Children of Israel in Egypt. There are no "parallels." The two stories are so full of contrasts that the only thing they have in common is the word "Egypt."

The fact that Luke omits the incident has no bearing on the correctness of Matthew's account. The argument from silence is always precarious. Luke is also silent, in Acts, about the journey of his friend Paul into Arabia. We should know nothing at all about that excursion were it not for the Apostle's own account (Galatians 1:17).

There are difficulties connected with the Flight into Egypt. However, they are not insurmountable, especially if we remember that the Gospels are outlines rather than full biographies.

* * * * *

In Old Testament times, Egypt was regarded as the rich granary of the ancient world. Hungry nomads, like Abraham, journeyed thither whenever their own lands were visited by famine (Genesis 12:10ff.). Whole tribes did likewise. The sons of Israel were thrilled when they discovered what an advantage it was for them to have their brother Joseph "over all the land of Egypt" (Genesis 41:41ff.). They had preferential treatment. Probably they needed it, because "all countries came into Egypt to Joseph for to buy corn; because the famine was sore in all the earth" (Genesis 41:57).

"Ephraim and Manasseh" (Genesis 46:20), were the sons of Joseph by his Egyptian wife Asenath, who was the daughter of Potipherah, the high priest at Heliopolis. Asenath was chosen to be Joseph's wife by Pharaoh himself (Genesis 41:45).

Most of the historical books contain numerous references to the land of the pyramids, a land that played an important role in the life of the small Jewish State. Palestine lay between two great powers — Assyria, Babylon, and then Syria to the North, and Egypt to the South. As a "buffer state," Palestine often felt the full force of their military might.

There are not many references to Egypt in the New Testament. There were Egyptians at Jerusalem for the Feast of Pentecost (Acts 2:10). Stephen summarized the experience of his nation in bondage to Pharaoh in his defense before the high priest (Acts 7). Paul was mistaken for an Egyptian insurrectionist (Acts 21:38). There is a vague and symbolic allusion to Egypt in the Apocalypse (Revelation 11:8).

The Flight was occasioned by a dream, following the departure of the Wise Men. In this dream, an angel warned Joseph that Herod would make an attempt on the Babe's life. The angel ordered him to take the family to Egypt, where they were to remain until the death of the tyrant (Matthew 2:13).

"Egypt has, in all ages, been the natural place of refuge for all who were driven from Palestine by distress, persecution, or discontent."[1]

[1] Dean Farrar, *The Life of Christ,* p. 19.

Tradition marks out the route which Joseph took into Egypt. It was through Hebron, Gaza, and the desert. This is the most direct way. The tradition is probably correct. At Hebron and at Gaza, visitors are still shown "the exact place" where the Holy Family is alleged to have rested.

Hebron, nineteen miles south-west of Jerusalem, is perhaps the oldest continuously inhabited city in Palestine. It was a long-established town in the days of Abraham, who had close associations with it (Genesis 13:18; 18:1ff.). Sarah died there (Genesis 23:2) and was buried in the cave of Machpelah, just outside (Genesis 23:17). This became the family vault of the Patriarchs and Matriarchs of Israel, the final resting-place of Abraham, Isaac, and Jacob, and of Sarah, Rebekah, and Leah (Genesis 49:31; 50:13). From the beginning of the Hebrew occupation of Palestine, there were six Cities of Refuge (Numbers 35:10ff.), originally designed to provide a haven for those guilty of involuntary manslaughter. These cities were: Shechem, Kadesh, Bezer, Ramoth Gilead, Golan, and Hebron (Joshua 20:7; 21:11; 1 Chronicles 6:55, 57). Hebron was the first capital of King David, who reigned over Judah for seven years before he transferred his headquarters to Jerusalem (2 Samuel 2:11; 5:5; 1 Kings 2:11). In spite of its long and complicated history, Hebron is not mentioned in the New Testament.

Gaza was the chief and southernmost of the five great Philistian cities, the other four being Ashkelon, Ashdod, Ekron, and Gath. Gaza was only three miles from the Mediterranean coast. It was the greatest trade center of Biblical Palestine. It had a stranglehold on the busy caravan highways, southwest to Egypt, south to Arabia by way of Beersheba, north to Damascus, southeast to Edom, and northeast to Jerusalem. It was the crossroads of the Middle East. Samson was imprisoned at Gaza. Here the Philistines made sport of him as he turned the huge grindstone in his blindness. Here, in the temple of the god Dagon, he revenged himself upon his enemies (Judges 16:21ff.). It was on the way to Gaza that Philip met the Ethiopian eunuch (Acts 8:26ff.), whose conversion led to the establishment of the Coptic Church — the oldest Church in Christendom.

The Holy Family traveled this ancient route on their life-or-death journey. They were exposed to perils of every description. There are some commentators who think that if our Lord uttered the words, "Pray ye that your flight be not in the winter" (Mark 13:18; cf. Matthew 24:20), they reflect what He had heard Mary and Joseph say they had endured in that night flight.

The marvel is not that it is a story of fear, privation, suffering and brutality. The marvel is that this little Child, barely saved from being murdered, was God's Word of Salvation to all men everywhere.

Philo (30 B.C.-A.D. 50), was the greatest philosopher the Jews gave to the ancient world. He was thoroughly versed in Greek scholarship. By the use of allegory, he transformed Biblical stories into philosophical principles. It was he who developed the doctrine of the *Logos,* with which many scholars claim the author of the Fourth Gospel was familiar.[2] Philo lived in Alexandria. He tells us that in his day there were more than a million Jews in Egypt. The great city of Alexandria was divided into five districts. Two of the five had a predominantly Jewish population.

There is a very ancient tradition which says the Holy Family stayed at Matarieh, the former Heliopolis, which is a few miles north-east from Cairo. This may have been the oldest city in Egypt. It was the original home of the sun-god. In Jeremiah (43:13), Heliopolis is called "Beth-shemish," which means "house of the sun." The high priest was also the chief astrologer, and at times his power exceeded that of Pharaoh. Matarieh

[2] I am deliberately indefinite in this statement because I incline to the view that John's source was Hebrew thought and tradition.

is also called On in the Old Testament (Genesis 41:45, 50; 46:20).

A group of obelisks stood in front of the great Temple of Re-Harakhte, god of the rising sun. Only one of these massive pillars remains in its original position. It is the oldest and perhaps the most beautiful pillar in all Egypt. It towers fifty-six feet above the encroaching Nile mud and carries a clear-cut hieroglyphic inscription concerning "Horus, son of the sun, beloved of the spirits of Heliopolis." Two of the obelisks from Matarieh are famous throughout the world as "Cleopatra's Needles." One of them stands on the Thames' embankment in London, and the other in New York's Central Park. Jesus may very well have seen them during the time He was a refugee.

Moses, who was reared by Pharaoh's daughter (Exodus 2:10), may perhaps have studied at Heliopolis. He was trained "in all the wisdom of the Egyptians" (Acts 7:22), which suggests that his schooling took place in the religious and cultural center of the empire. The priests of On were so renowned for their learning that Plato is said to have visited them.

Economic depression seems to have hit the area at the beginning of the Roman era. Matarieh was probably little more than a ghost town when Joseph and Mary found shelter there for the Child. Most of the city was abandoned. Briars covered the heaps of rubbish, and jackals made their lairs in the ruined splendors.

The amazing Apocryphal Gospels have had a field day with the Flight into Egypt. As the Holy Trio go their way, the miraculous accompanies them at every step. The repetition becomes ludicrous.

In these fables, lions, dragons, and panthers adore the infant Jesus. His Mother is hungry, so He speaks to a palm tree, and it immediately bends down so she may eat its fruit

In one temple they visit, three hundred fifty idols bow down before the Mother and her Child. (No explanation is given of why pious Jews defile themselves by entering a pagan sanctuary.) In another story, they are chased from the house of a wealthy widow who had befriended them, because "the superstitious natives" fear the Child when He brings to life a dried and salted fish!

As they are traveling through the desert, they are accosted by two bandits names Titus and Dumachus. Titus bribes Damachus not to molest them. Straightway the Child sits up and foretells His Crucifixion, at Jerusalem a generation later, between two robbers — these two robbers. He promises Titus he will accompany Him to Paradise.

The myths are legion and ridiculous. The more they are compared with the sober stories of the New Testament, the more we can believe that at any rate some of the Councils of the Church have been under the over-ruling hand of God.

* * * * *

The angels had hardly sung their song of Peace and Goodwill before the soldiers of Herod went forth under those same stars on their errand of blood. The joy of the Magi was succeeded by the weeping of them that refused to be comforted. Jesus Himself, it is true, escaped to become the Great Innocent Sufferer of all time, but no wealth of love availed to delight these other innocent ones. Fear and force failed in their design, but they filled peaceful Bethlehem with the wail of frenzied women, whose murdered children would never come back to them.

His first procession through this world which He had come to save was, as it were, to flee along blood-stained streets, where the innocent were made to suffer at the hands of the enthroned bully, and quiet offenseless women had to bear that sharp and awful throe from which no mother's heart ever quite recovers.

The Slaughter of the Innocents shocks us. We are not appeased when we learn that the number of children involved was, in all probability, not very great, somewhere in the region of twenty. It is not the extent of the crime, but its very conception, which nauseates us. It is all thoroughly monstrous.

It was a mere bagatelle to Herod. It was not conspicuous among his other sadistic actions. It is quite in keeping with his known character. Josephus says of him, "he was brutish, and a stranger to all humanity."[3] Before he died, his name had become a low byword even among low people.

When it became known that Herod's days were numbered, most of the Jews were cautious enough not to express their relief publicly. But some hot-headed students in Jerusalem were so carried away with the news they hastened to remove the golden eagle from the gate of the Temple.

This was reported to the dying king, who was delirious and so enveloped by monstrous fancies and mis-shapen dreams that he was on the verge of suicide. Somehow the message got through to him and he recovered sufficiently to make the journey from Jericho to Jerusalem. So dynamic was his anger that he took a new lease on life. So determined was he to punish the offenders that he gained strength with every mile he traveled. Once he had arrived at the Holy City, the accused were paraded before him, and he poured out his wrath upon them. Forty students and two of their teachers, Rabbi Judas and Rabbi Matthias, were burned to death on his orders.

It was a perfectly natural reaction for him to express his fear and wrath in wholesale and indiscriminate destruction. The fact that *children* were the objects of his fury would have no bearing on the case at all. "Herod the Butcher" is an apt description of him.

"Herod will seek the young child to destroy him" (Matthew

[3] *Antiquities,* 17:6:5.

2:13). Herod will drench his hands anew with innocent blood. All the vile means which are available he will use. But he will fail to achieve his purpose, for he has made just one common error. He has drawn his plans and has estimated the rival forces, but he has not reckoned with God.

* * * * *

A voice was heard in Ramah,
Lamentation, and weeping, and great mourning,
Rachel weeping for her children,
And she would not be comforted, because they are not.

—Jeremiah 31:15; Matthew 2:18

Ramah was a village on the border of that portion of Palestine which belonged to the tribe of Benjamin (Joshua 18:25; 1 Kings 15:17ff.). It was situated on a highway between Bethel and "Ephrath, which is Bethlehem" (Genesis 35:19). It was at Ramah that Deborah judged Israel beneath the famous palm tree (Judges 4:5). There Jacob buried Rachel when she died giving birth to Benjamin. As she expired, she named her new-born *Ben-oni,* which means "son of my sorrow," but Jacob called him *Benjamin,* which means "son of my right hand" (Genesis 35:18).

Her tomb by the wayside became a national shrine. To the vivid religious imagination of the Jews, Rachel was a mother for Israel in all times and in all circumstances. She was sympathetic in all her children's misfortunes.

Jeremiah lived in a world of displaced persons. It seemed to his acutely sensitive soul that as the Exiles passed Rachel's Tomb on their forced march to Babylon under Nebuchadnezzar, he could hear her weeping for her children's woes.

In the lamentation over the Slaughter of the Innocents — the first Christian Martyrs — the Evangelist heard again Rachel weeping for her children.

* * * * *

According to Matthew, Joseph was instructed to remain in Egypt until God sent him word (Matthew 2:13). Apparently this summons was sent as soon as Herod died.

Considering that the Jews were so numerous in Egypt, and the constant communication between the two countries, the news of Herod's death must soon have reached him in the ordinary way. However, it was first made known to him by the angel (Matthew 2:19f.).

Joseph's obedience was instantaneous. He set off home without delay. Evidently he made no inquiries locally. He did not know that Archelaus was Herod's successor until he came into the land of Israel (Matthew 2:22).

Archelaus was ethnarch, or viceroy, of Judea, Samaria, and Idumea from 4 B.C. to A.D. 6. Then his disgusted subjects requested his removal. Jesus may well have based His parable of the pounds on this recent bit of Jewish history (cf. Luke 19:12ff.). Archelaus was banished to Gaul, and Judea had its first experience of Roman procurators. These were imperial officers who were appointed to trouble spots in the Empire by the Emperor himself. There were six of them between A.D. 6 and A.D. 41, when Herod Agrippa, grandson of Herod the Great, was made King of Judea by his friend Caligula, the mad Emperor who appointed his horse to a consulship.

When Joseph was directed to go into Egypt, he was not told to what place he should return (Matthew 2:13). Afterwards, when he was ordered home, the place was not designated (Matthew 2:20). It is plain, however, that he did not plan to travel to Nazareth. He evidently regarded Bethlehem, the City of David, as the proper place in which to rear the Son of David. He naturally supposed that He who was of the tribe of Judah should dwell in the land of Judah. This was the most sacred part of Palestine. No doubt, too, it was his idea that the promised Messiah ought to be brought up as near as possible to the Temple, where He might have frequent intercourse with the great priests and rabbis. Only through a special command of God was Joseph led to return with Jesus to Galilee (Matthew 2:22f.).

The fact that he made his abode in the upland city of Nazareth can be explained only on the assumption (about which Matthew is wholly silent) that this had been his earlier residence, as related by the Third Evangelist (Luke 1:26f.).

5

Where Two Worlds Meet

O world invisible, we view thee,
O world intangible, we touch thee,
O world unknowable, we know thee,
Inapprehensible, we clutch thee.

—Francis Thompson

THE WAY IN WHICH WE CELEBRATE CHRISTMAS IS AS strong a test of our religion as any to which we could submit.

It may be that we have been robbed of the beauty and simplicity of our traditional Christmas. It may also be that we did not put up much of a fight to retain it.

Lavish spending and giving, to ourselves and to our friends, has reached the crazy stage where the whole business of presents is, perhaps, the worst headache of the entire year. It is alleged that the mother of a Southern belle, when asked by her daughter, "What do you give a man who has everything?" replied, "Encouragement, dear, encouragement!"

The Wise Men offered gifts, and people have been doing it

ever since. We have forgotten that the Magi were not the originators. Man did not start this giving spree. God did. God began it all with a Gift that is beyond words. It caused the Apostle to exclaim, "Thanks be to God for his unspeakable gift" (2 Corinthians 9:15).

When I was a boy, we used to hang up our stockings at the high mahogany mantelpiece of my grandfather's queer old house. I remember quite clearly the year we graduated from stockings in the living-room to pillow-cases in the bedrooms. I remember it so vividly because three of the Aunties thought it their solemn duty to inform us of the terrible things that happen to children who are greedy, selfish and ungrateful.

Cousin Ronald almost quaked with fear. He was an outgoing, ambitious boy, rather large for his age. His size was not concealed by the sickly puce breeches he wore on special occasions. He had a strong voice and a good memory, and he never needed a second invitation to recite in public. The Aunties thought it was remarkable that he could be heard at the back of the sanctuary. They considered this a sign that Ronald was something special, and they treated him accordingly. This particular Christmas he had concocted the heinous idea of fastening a folded sheet to the bottom of his bed, in lieu of a pillow-case. After the dire warnings had been repeated three times, Ronald used his weight to make me promise not to breathe a word to anyone about his wicked scheme. He was rather subdued for the rest of the vacation, which was very strange for him. His mother thought he was "coming down with something." The Aunties suspected he had eaten too many candies. Cousin Connie looked down her nose at him and wafted by with that touch of aloofness only dainty little girls can achieve.

We seem to have gone berserk in the matter of presents. We badly need a new sense of proportion, or, better still, an inspired sense of discernment, which will get us back on an even keel. We must learn to distinguish the reality from the trappings. It is a sad commentary on our day to have to admit there are hosts of people who think their best friends are those who give them the most expensive presents.

The gifts we make to one another have little meaning unless they are related to the Grace of our Lord Jesus Christ, who, though He was rich, yet for our sakes became poor, that we, through His poverty, might have eternal riches (2 Corinthians 8:9).

At Christmas we are judged. We are not, however, judged by the presents we give, any more than we are judged by the presents we receive. At Christmas we are judged by the Christ-Child in our midst. He does not judge our goodness. He does not judge our moral character. He takes no account of the fact that we belong to a Church which bears His name. He does not call for the books to be opened. The Christ-Child in our midst judges us according to our recognition of His presence and according to the welcome we extend to Him. That means, in effect, that the Christ-Child does not judge us at all. He brings us to the place where we judge ourselves in His light. That is the ultimate and final form of judgment, from which there is no appeal.

Do *we* recognize the presence of the Christ-Child in our midst and accord Him the welcome He deserves? Do *we,* this Christmas, hear in our hearts strange, celestial music, "a filmy melody, like a star-beam," streaming out of the throne of Almighty God, announcing the birth of a Baby? Do *we* understand that the Baby whose birth we so noisily celebrate is *the Lord Jesus Christ?*

Christos, in Greek, means "the Anointed." Christmas is the Festival of the Anointed. In Hebrew it is *Messiah,* the sublime title which embodied and expressed all Jewish hopes and longings.

This Christ-Child is the Lord Messiah. He is tiny and frail in body and lowly in estate. He is Love Incarnate.

* * * * *

Bethlehem is much more than a geographical location. It is the spot "Where Two Worlds Meet." "Love came down at Christmas," sings the poet. "The Word became flesh and dwelt among us," says John.

We see the Babe, weak and helpless and small, but we must not lose our perspective. We must not forget, even at Christmas — *especially* at Christmas — that this Love will become flaming, revolutionary, triumphant. *Especially* at Christmas must we face realistically the vital, elemental truth that this Love Incarnate — and so Christmas itself — is related to the sit-in demonstrations and the marches in the Deep South; to the bitter racial strife of the industrial North; to the bruised and broken spirits of the people behind the Iron Curtain; to the oppressed people in Cuba; to the hungry displaced persons in the Near East and in the Far East; to those who, directly or indirectly, are responsible for their displacement; and to all who seek to profit from man's inhumanity to man. What it says about these issues may not bring *comfort* to either side, but it will bring the assurance that the fabric of the world is woven by God; that this is a Moral Universe; that *we* do not have the last word and the deciding vote; that, in fact, "the Lord God omnipotent reigneth" (Revelation 19:16).

Because He lies helpless in a stable, we need reminding that He was

Born a Child and yet a King,

that He will overcome principalities and powers, making a show of them openly (Colossians 2:15).

Yet this Revolutionary Peasant is the Prince of Peace (Isaiah 9:6). He was born because men did not know the things that belonged to their peace. He came from God to bring men to God. Clement of Alexandria knew this when he said, so boldly, that the Divine became human in order that the human might become Divine.

And we the life of God shall know,
For God is manifest below.

He came not only to preach "peace to you which were afar off, and to them that were nigh" (Ephesians 2:17), but to make that peace possible. Indeed, "He is our peace" (Ephesians 2:14).

Who could have dreamed that the Child lying on the coarse hay would have so sorely troubled the luxury-loving Herod? Who could have dreamed that this Unknown Infant would have presented the illustrious Roman governor, Pontius Pilate, with the weightiest problem of his public career? Who could have dreamed that this poverty-encircled Child would have defeated the Emperor Julian more than three-hundred years later? Who would have been foolish enough to prophesy that He would be worshipped by countless millions throughout the centuries? Who would have dared to say that because of this humble Babe the universal institution of slavery would be abolished, and the highest ethical and moral ideals proclaimed?

There is nothing to account for these things except that, in the infinite wisdom and grace of God, Bethlehem was the focal-point, the meeting-place of two worlds.

The temporal was exalted by its union with the Eternal. The stable suddenly became a palace. An outcast Child was King of kings. A Babe revealed that gladness is at the heart of things.

Simplicity and Immeasurable Love are on the throne. Everything else is upon its knees. God is speaking my language, and yours, and every man's It is so simple that poor shepherds can understand. It is so profound that the wisest of men will always be learning.

* * * * *

Where Two Worlds Meet

Every time we think of the Incarnation, new difficulties and fresh problems arise. Questions force themselves upon us. We are made to approach the subject from different angles, and to look at it in a new light. It may be a long time before the answers begin to appear, but only a fool resents the questions. If we do not know the answer, that is all the more reason why the question should be asked.

How is it possible to conceive of a God "outside" the Universe, when there is no "outside"? When the answer to this question is understood, how can we explain what we mean when we talk about God "sending His Son into the world"? Is there any real justification for speaking of Bethlehem as the place "Where Two Worlds Meet"?

The Son of God cannot come into the world as if from without, because He is already in the world as its Creator and Sustainer (Colossians 1:16f.; Ephesians 3:9ff.; Hebrews 1:1ff.; John 1:3, 10). But He can come *in a new way,* in the full expression of what He essentially is. He can "enter" as a recognizable Personality.

God was never absent from the world so that He needed at some moment of time to come into it. He was always here. God is Perfect Being, and Perfect Being is Perfect Love. Just because it is perfect, it can never keep itself to itself, but must be forever giving itself to its creation. This is the significance of the Old Testament. It shows how God was progressively entering into history. But God is, above all, Ethical Being — Holy Love — and it was the Divine ethical self-giving that reached its culmination in Christ.

The bare fact that Jesus was born in Bethlehem of Judea in the days of Herod the king was a declaration of kinship, for He was the Son of God, and might have seemed parted from men by an unbridged chasm. But "the Word was made flesh," and with that, the half-forgotten truth that man was made at first in the image of God (Genesis 1:26f.) was reasserted. Between God and man there is not contrast merely. There is substantial and profound resemblance. The Son of God did not cease to be Divine in becoming man.

In Christ we have the *unity* of the Divine and the human. In Him they were *one*. It was not a *union*. It was a *unity*. There were not "two natures" in Christ. There was one essential ethical nature in one Divine-human Person. Jesus did not possess a double consciousness or a split personality. He had a single consciousness of Sonship towards God in the most perfectly integrated personality this world has ever known. The Man who appears before us in the Gospels always manifests this attitude towards God as Father. But such consciousness of Sonship was *at once Divine and human*. In it we have the point where the Divine and the human meet and are one. So there is a place "Where Two Worlds Meet."

Many times in history, people who have prided themselves on being "spiritually minded" have argued that Jesus did not come down to our level, that He never really "became man." If God *could not* become man, then the finite would constitute such a limitation to the infinite as to deny the very idea of God.

To the Greeks, the idea of an Incarnate God was foolishness. To the Jews, it was a stumbling-block. Even within the early Church there were heretics who did not believe that Jesus was a real human being. That is why the Fourth Evangelist was so careful, deliberate and emphatic, "The Word became flesh and dwelt among us" (John 1:14). That is also why he wrote his First Epistle.

Little Jesus, wast Thou shy
Once, and just so small as I?
And what did it feel like to be
Out of heaven, and just like me?

—Francis Thompson

WHERE TWO WORLDS MEET

I believe . . . in Jesus Christ, His only Son, our Lord;
who was conceived by the Holy Ghost;
born of the Virgin
Mary.

I believe that He who was "very God of very God" in truth took our nature upon Him, and was made "very Man of very man." I believe it because I know a place "Where Two Worlds Meet."

* * * * *

When the angels of heaven met the shepherds of earth in King David's pasture outside Bethlehem, these shepherds were given a sign. Have you ever wondered why the shepherds needed a sign? Why couldn't they go straight into the city they knew so intimately, pick out the Holy Child, and worship Him? Why did they have to be told?

The answer is that without a sign they would never have found what they were seeking. They knew that Messiah would come. They had not the slightest idea *how* He would come.

So the angel, in effect, said to them, "It's no use looking in the homes of the rich, or even in the hovels of the poor, because the Child you seek will be born in a stable and laid in a manger!" For once they got their directions straight. "They found the Babe, lying in a manger" (Luke 2:16).

The manger is an integral part of the Christmas picture. As we look upon that simple, familiar, precious scene, we see not only the ever-repeated marvel of a new life, but the Son of God, the Word made flesh, come to dwell with us, full of Grace and Truth (John 1:14). We are not able to fathom the Divine mysteries, but here, we know, somehow, Two Worlds Meet.

To reach Christmas, the amazing Hinge of Time, we must tread the path of wonder and awe, for this is the Lord's doing, and it is marvelous in our eyes.

Stand amazed, ye heavens, at this:
See the Lord of earth and skies;
Humbled to the dust He is,
And in a manger lies.

—Charles Wesley

We must tread this reverent path joyfully, with hearts filled with gratitude that we are the objects of such a matchless Love.

This Christmas, let us express our thankfulness to Him who spared not His own Son, but freely delivered Him up for us all, and with Him also freely gives us all things (Romans 8:32).

Let us show this gratitude by remembering that He came down to our level so that the homage of our hearts may be laid at His feet. Whatever presents we give to our friends this Christmas, let us bring to Him the gift of our hearts.

* * * * *

If we do, He will call us to accept the Christmas purpose: "Peace on earth among men of good will" (Luke 2:14). His call will be a challenge, because the only possible way we can really respond is to become men of goodwill ourselves — *men of goodwill for all of God's children everywhere.* If we believe that God made all men, and not just "us," we cannot be related to God without also being related to them.

Goodwill is in constant danger of crumbling unless it is fortified by the spirit of God's own goodwill, that is to say, unless we have the mind of Christ, and can say,

> *For God so loved the world that he gave his*
> *only begotten Son, that whosoever believeth*
> *in him should not perish, but have*
> *everlasting life* (John 3:16).

It would be much easier to understand and accept that great verse if it said, "God so loved Israel," or "God so loved the Church." It would be much more acceptable if it left out that awful word "whosoever." It would be much easier to appreciate it if we did not know that whenever John speaks of "the world," he means "the rebellious world, organized against God." But the word "whosoever" is there, and it states flatly, "God so loved *the world,*" and that must mean *everybody in it.*

The Christmas message is for everyone. Perhaps that is why Incarnate God came as "one of the masses." Never came a king in such a great humility. There was no fanfare of trumpets, no parade of outward pomp, no twenty-one-gun salute. Alice Meynell has sung of the coming of Jesus,

No sudden thing of glory and fear
Was the Lord's coming; but the dear
Slow nature's days followed each other
To form the Saviour from His Mother,
One of the children of the year.

Many children were born that year. Jesus was one of them. He came into the world as all other babies come. He came as one of us, so that He could appeal to all of us.

The "good tidings of great joy" are for "all the people" (Luke 2:10). We cannot limit our goodwill to our own folks and be the enemy of those who live in other lands or of those who happen to be born of a different race. We cannot limit our goodwill if we want to celebrate the Festival in spirit and in truth.

In this respect we would all do well to realize that there is a sense in which it is wrong to speak glibly of Christ as a Jew who belonged to one particular nationality at one specific period of time.

In Bethlehem, we see the Child who was "the Son of Man," "with a heart pulsing with the blood of the human race." Somehow, we do not feel that His difference in national origin, in time, in climate, or in custom, estranges Him from us. In Him there is no narrow nationalism, no class prejudice, no "master-race" pride, but only a love which embraces the whole of mankind.

His words may be translated into any language. They *belong* to every tribe that hears them. They cannot belong *exclusively* to any people. They will always belong to the whole wide world. He is the link between God and *all* people. He is not the Mediator between God and a particular nation. So the story of Bethlehem belongs to every home, and is told in every tongue.

The catholicity of our carols illustrates this. They come, not only from different communions, but also from varied nationalities. Think of some of the best known. "*Adeste Fideles*" was written by an anonymous Frenchman in the early part of the eighteenth century for use in the private chapel of a wealthy Roman Catholic family. "O Little Town of Bethlehem" was written by the Prince of American Preachers, Bishop Phillips Brooks, in 1867; it was first sung in Trinity Church, Boston. "It Came Upon the Midnight Clear" is the only Christmas hymn ever written by a Unitarian, Rev. Edmund Hamilton Sears, also of Massachusetts. "Hark! The Herald Angels Sing" is perhaps the most popular carol ever written. The Englishman Charles Wesley wrote the words, and the German composer Mendelssohn wrote the tune. "Silent Night! Holy Night!" was written by the German Lutheran Pastor, Rev. Joseph Mohr in 1818. The most distinguished Congregational Minister of the eighteenth century, Isaac Watts, wrote "Joy to the World" in 1719, while the tune "Antioch" is by the great German composer George Frederick Handel and is, perhaps, the best example of a fugue tune in any hymnal. In this almost casual selection we have represented France, America, Germany, and England, and the following churches: Roman Catholic, Methodist, Unitarian, Lutheran, Episcopalian, and Congregationalist.

The idyl of Bethlehem can be told by "mothers of Salem"

in Palestine or Massachusetts. There is a universality in Christ which leaves none out. Bethlehem, Pa., means as much to Him as Bethlehem, Judea.

Have we so easily forgotten what kind of love came down at Christmas? Does the careful deliberation with which we limit our intimate circle, and restrict our presents to them, blind us to the essential fact that God has no favorites?

At Christmas time, what do we do with these difficult words of Jesus, "If ye love them which love you, what reward have ye? do not even the publicans the same? And if ye salute your brethren only, what do ye more than others? do not even the publicans so?" (Matthew 5:46f.). If prejudice has usurped the place of thought, there is not a great deal we can do with them. Self-centeredness is a crippling disease.

Exclusiveness is the deadly foe of philanthropy. Its mean spirit is finely voiced in Tennyson's "Place of Art," where the solitary soul, looking through Oriel windows, can speak of men as "swine,"

O, God-like isolation which art mine,
I can but count thee perfect gain:
What time I watch the darkening droves of swine
That range on yonder plain.

In contrast to this, John Oxenham wrote,

Am I my brother's keeper?
Yes, of a truth!
Thine asking is thine answer.
That self-condemning cry of Cain
Has been the plea of every selfish soul since then,
Which hath its brother slain.
God's word is plain,
And doth thy shrinking soul arraign.
Thy brother's keeper?
Yea, of a truth thou art!

For if not — who?
Are ye not both, — both thou and he,
Of God's great family?
How rid thee of thy soul's responsibility?
For every ill in all the world
Each soul is sponsor and account must bear.
And He, and he thy brother of despair,
Claim, of thy overmuch, their share.
Thou hast had good, and he the strangled days;
But now, — the old things pass.
No longer of thy grace
Is he content to live in evil case
For the anointing of thy shining face.
The old things pass. — Beware lest ye pass with them,
And your place
Become an emptiness.[1]

The secret of ultimate harmony is offered to us at Christmas. In Bethlehem we find the Son of Man like unto the Son of God. He does not rule the world from a high and lofty throne, to which only the most exalted can climb, but from a modest cradle, before which all may kneel.

One morning, when I entered my office, I found that an unknown friend had slipped this paragraph by Margaret Carey under the door:

> While substitute teaching in a Junior High School, I found a book, and recognized the boy's name written in it. When I gave it to him, he said, "No. This belongs to my brother, — he's half-a-grade ahead of me because he's six months older than I am." Before I recovered from this remark, he added, "One of us is adopted, but I forget which one." The words lifted my spirits as I

[1] *The King's High Way*, p. 67.

visualized the home where being adopted made so little difference.

When I read that, I thought, Here is a home where the spirit of Christmas really is manifest. We would not go far wrong in calling it "an ideal home" — and if we do, cannot we go a step further, and see that this is the very spirit which is needed in the world today?

Instead of thanking God that we are not as other men are, which all too often we do, Christmas bids us recognize that other men are basically like us. We all have the same hopes that uplift, the same spirit that animates, and the same confidence that encourages.

The secret of ultimate harmony is to be found "Where Two Worlds Meet." "Let us now go even unto Bethlehem" (Luke 2:15), and as we accompany the shepherds — in haste — let us not be so hasty that we miss the message,

The hopes and fears of all the years
Are met in thee to-night

—Phillips Brooks

6

Sinai and Bethlehem

THE OLD TESTAMENT CONTAINS A VIVID DESCRIPTION OF Moses receiving the Law on Mount Sinai:

> *It came to pass, on the third day,*
> *when it was morning, that there were*
> *thunders and lightnings, and a thick*
> *cloud upon the mount, and the voice*
> *of a trumpet exceeding loud; and all*
> *the people that were in the camp trembled. . . .*
> *And mount Sinai was altogether on smoke,*
> *because the Lord descended on it in fire;*
> *and the smoke thereof ascended as the*
> *smoke of a furnace, and the whole mount*
> *quaked greatly* (Exodus 19:16ff.).

In the New Testament there is an equally vivid description of a totally different kind of event in the city of David,

> *And it came to pass, while they were there,*
> *the days were fulfilled that she should be*

> *delivered. And she brought forth her first-born son; and wrapped him in swaddling clothes, and laid him in a manger, because there was no room for them in the inn* (Luke 2:6f.).

The contrast between the giving of the Law on Sinai's famous hill, and the coming of the Prince of glory in the stinking stable of an inn, could hardly be greater. Yet it is certainly no greater than the difference between the Lawgiver and the Messiah, or between the Law and the Gospel. "The law was given through Moses, grace and truth came in Jesus Christ" (John 1:17).

The system of the Law was given through a man. It was given through an agent. It was given through a purely human figure. It was given through a frail being who himself failed to live up to all the demands of the revelation he received (cf., e.g., Numbers 20). It is not difficult to imagine the Law being given through any one of a dozen outstanding Old Testament characters, from Abraham to Amos.

The Gospel is the Good News of God revealing Himself *in* Jesus, so that *in Him* He might reconcile the world unto Himself (2 Corinthians 5:19). It is not merely personal. It is peculiarly personal. It is impossible to think of the Gospel apart from Him in whom it came into the world. It is this personal element that distinguishes Christianity. You may accept Buddhism or Confucianism without concerning yourself with Buddha or Confucius. You cannot accept Christianity without accepting Christ.

Christianity *is* Christ. Others have said, "I *teach* the truth." Jesus said, "I *am* . . . the truth" (John 14:6). That is why we insist upon the finality of God's Self-revelation in His Son. Theologies come and go, but the Gospel shines on with undiminishing splendor. Creedal statements change with changing times, but the Truth they are intended to describe endures unchanged. That is why we say *it is impossible to think of the Gospel apart from Him in whom it came into the world.*

Christ *is* the Gospel. *He* is the Good News. He is the Son in whom the Father reveals Himself. In the Son we see the Father both infinitely loving and infinitely lovable. In Him "the grace of God hath appeared, bringing salvation to all men" (Titus 2:11).

This poor, despised working-man of Nazareth "appeared" for the brief space of some thirty-three years. He lived under appalling conditions, in a small country, among an obscure people. He remained silent and hidden for thirty out of the thirty-three years. He never traveled a hundred miles from the place where He was born. Yet His appearing has had consequences through all history, and up into the eternities, that we can never describe, and has bequeathed to humanity permanent and universal values that we can never exhaust. But they all root themselves in this, that Jesus was the only begotten of the Father, who came from the bosom of the Father, and is therefore the perfect revelation of the heart and mind of God (cf. John 1:18). This gives Him universal worth and permanent value. In the personal coming of Christ into humanity, God's "Grace and Truth" came in the fullness of their glory.

"The Law was given *through* Moses." It was a revelation of God no different in kind from other partial and imperfect revelations which the Old Testament records as having come to men at special times and for special purposes. It was different in degree.

The giving of the Law was a milestone in human history. It elevated man's conception of God. It revolutionized his relationship to his fellows. Yet it was a finite revelation. It was limited and conditioned by the ability of Moses to receive, understand, and interpret it.

"Grace and Truth" — the full and final revelation of God's

free Love, the unique combination which could be expressed in no other way and through no merely human medium — "came in Jesus Christ."

Moses transmitted the Hebrew faith by his revelation of the Divine Oneness. But the revelation of the Eternal Will, momentous as it is in itself and sublime as its results are, fails to meet our deepest needs. It does not even make missionaries and Reformers out of us.

But in Jesus Christ — and only in Him — we receive the Grace of God. There is no Grace, in the full meaning of that glorious word, apart from Him who gave Himself for us that He might redeem us from all evil, make us His own peculiar possession, and flood us with the forces that work for the salvation and progress of the human race. Jesus alone takes us within the Divine Mind. In seeing Him we see the Father. The supreme significance of Grace is that in it *we no longer stand outside God.*

Through the ages prior to the coming of Jesus, that Grace had not appeared in its fullness. The Law came by Moses, but not *Grace* — not the very Truth and Reality of God. The just claims of God on the trust and obedience of men were fully expressed on Mount Sinai, but nothing was said about "the free gift of God" to men of abundant pardon and all-sufficient strength.

> *God, who, at sundry times and in divers manners,*
> *spake in time past unto the fathers by the prophets,*
> *hath, in these last days, spoken unto us in His Son*
> (Hebrews 1:1).

* * * * *

"The law was given through Moses; grace and truth came in Jesus Christ" (John 1:17). Here we have three key-words of the Bible. *Law* is a key-word of the Old Testament. *Grace* is a key-word of the Epistles. *Truth* is a key-word in the writings of "the disciple whom Jesus loved."

The proper human response to Law is obedience. The Law *demands* obedience from us — "or else." The Law gives us no choice. It prescribes the path of duty. It says, "Thou shalt," and, equally dogmatically, it says, "Thou shalt not." The Law is centered in man. It is related to what *I* do. The Law speaks only through symbols. At best it gives us "a shadow of good things to come" (Hebrews 10:1). A man may observe the Law in his conduct without being in any degree spiritual in his nature.

In the eyes of the Law we are citizens. The Law is administered by an impartial judge. He must not be related to any with whom he deals. He is not interested in the individual. His only concern is to uphold the Law. President Eisenhower summed it all up when he sent federal troops to Little Rock with the statement, "The Law is more important than people." This is the philosophy of the Old Testament.

Grace is God's Love in action — stooping, seeking, giving itself without limit, that the object of its Love, however unworthy, might be redeemed. Grace says, "The Law was made for man, and not man for the Law" (cf. Mark 2:27). The Jew was the prisoner of the Law. The New Testament makes Grace all-important. Gerard Manley Hopkins caught its spirit when he wrote,

> *I say that we are wound*
> *With mercy round and round,*
> *As if with air.*

There is only one adequate response to such Grace, and that is — it must be — love.

And yet, because it is Grace, and not Law, it does not *demand* our love. It *requests* it. The imperative does not come from without but from within. It does not say "You must." It says "You may." It seeks not a master-slave, or judge-prisoner, relationship, but a gracious personal fellowship. In the mystery of God's Grace, we are free to withhold the love He seeks. "Behold, I stand at the door and knock" (Revelation 3:20) is the word of Grace. Grace does not break in. It does not violate our personality.

Grace is Divine. It is centered in God. Its essence is not what *I* do, but what *God* has done for me in Jesus Christ. In the eyes of Grace we are not *citizens,* we are *children.* Grace depends upon an intimate personal relationship. It is the Father's concern for His family. Grace does not come through symbols. It comes in Reality. It is not the shadow of good things to come. It is the substance of the Highest, and has already come.

Grace does not come *through* an *agent*, but *in* a *Son,* in whom "dwelleth all the fulness of the Godhead bodily" (Colossians 2:9). He is, indeed, "the only begotten Son of God" (John 3:18), who alone can say, "I and my Father are one" (John 10:30).

Jesus did not become the Son of God at His Incarnation or at His baptism in the same way that John says men become "the sons of God" by believing on His name (John 1:12). He did not become a Son in the stable, for even there He revealed the glory which He had with His Father before the world was (John 17:5).

> *In the beginning was the Word, and the*
> *Word was with God, and the Word was God*
> *. . . . And the Word became flesh and*
> *dwelt among us, full of Grace and Truth*
> (John 1:1, 14).

* * * * *

If the only proper response to Law is obedience, and the only proper response to Grace is love, then the only proper response to Truth is *faith.*

The idea of Truth seems to dominate the mind of the Fourth Evangelist. He never mentions "Grace" again in the Gospel, but he has so much to say about "Truth" that you might be excused for thinking he wrote this book to answer Pilate's question, "What is truth?" (John 18:38).

John records that Jesus described His mission in these words, "For this purpose was I born, and for this purpose came I into the world, that I should bear witness to the truth" (John 18:37).

When the fickle crowds rejected Him, Jesus said to them, "Because I say the truth, ye believe me not" (John 8:45). He claimed to be "a man that told you the truth" (John 8:40). He assured His disciples, "I am . . . the truth" (John 14:6).

It is said that each country has its "earthquake zone." This is a well-defined area especially susceptible to shocks. Let an earthquake occur in Japan, and if its effects are felt at all in this country, they will be felt first within this particular area. The reason for this is what geologists call a "fault," a displacement of strata in the earth's crust.

All human philosophies have a fault, a fatal weakness somewhere. They can look good under fair conditions. But under the shocks of life, the tragic upheavals caused by sin, suffering, and death, human philosophies go to pieces, and those who trusted in them find they have no solid ground on which to stand. In the final analysis, humanity has only one firm foundation: "I am the truth." "As the truth is in Jesus" (Ephesians 4:21) — there is no fault there. There is no latent weakness in Him. This was the basis of Paul's great confidence, "I am persuaded that neither death nor life . . . shall be able to separate us from the love of God, which is in Christ Jesus our Lord" (Romans 8:38f.).

Because Jesus is the Truth, He promised to give "the Spirit of truth" (John 15:26; 14:17), to guide the faithful "into all the truth" (John 16:13). Those who open their hearts to

Him will not only "know the truth," but the Truth shall make them free (John 8:32).

On the night in which He was betrayed, Jesus prayed for His disciples. Judas had disappeared on his ghastly errand. The rest of them seem to have been in a daze. Christ's petition for His friends was that they might be "sanctified in the truth" (John 17:7). He considered this so very important that He asked it twice in the same prayer (John 17:9). Where Truth is, there is the Gospel. Where people are "sanctified in the truth," there is the Church.

* * * * *

There is significance in the fact that these two words "Grace" and "Truth" are in such close combination. What God hath joined together, let no man put asunder.

Truth, by itself, might be something harsh and forbidding. Truth, by itself, might be bleak and unfriendly. Truth, by itself, might come in only to condemn. So the Apostle was careful to exhort his converts to speak "the truth in love" (Ephesians 4:15).

Grace, by itself, might be misunderstood to be a light and shallow thing. Grace, by itself, might appear to be blind to the facts. Grace, by itself, might seem unable to deal adequately with the gross realities of the total situation. Grace, by itself, might be thought to free us from the guilt of sin, without doing anything about its power.

Jesus comes to us at Christmas neither as the stark Truth from which we seek to hide, nor as a doting Santa Claus. He comes to us "full of grace *and* truth."

He brings us face to face with Truth as it really is. For the first time we see Truth embodied in a Personality. For the first time the light of the Divine Truth is focused like a perfect X-ray machine upon our hearts and lives. There is no more hiding of the facts about ourselves or the facts about this world. "He was in the world, and the world was made by him, but the world knew him not" (John 1:10). Nevertheless, He knew the truth about the world. "This is the judgment, that the light is come into the world, and men loved darkness rather than the light, because their deeds were evil" (John 3:19). This diagnosis is accurate. It is not flattering. "The whole world lieth in the evil one" (1 John 5:19).

But the Truth is matched with an equal Grace. It is Grace which deals with the facts Truth exposes. So, in Jesus, an older word comes true,

Mercy and truth are met together;
Righteousness and peace have kissed each other
(Psalm 85:10).

Yet John's word "grace" is greater than the Psalmist's "mercy." Mercy might be only a remission of the sinner's penalty, as when an earthly ruler grants a general amnesty. Grace is Love which is not satisfied with forgiveness, but must press on to redeem, reclaim, and restore.

Hark! a voice from yonder manger,
Soft and sweet, doth entreat,
Flee from woe and danger;
Brethren, come; from all that grieves you
You are freed; all you need
I will surely give you.

—Paul Gerhardt

"Grace and Truth" confronted men when Jesus was here on earth. He brought them face to face with the Truth which was Himself. He showed them God. He showed them Divine Love and Divine Holiness, not as distinct and separate entities, here the Divine Love and there the Divine Holiness; but as integrated Holy Love. In God there is no Holiness that is not *Loving* Holiness, and there is no Love that is not *Holy* Love.

There can be no revelation of God apart from a revelation

of self. Every clearer glance we get into the nature of God brings with it a corresponding insight into our own characters. When Jesus showed men the Holy Love of God, they saw their own sin too. He broke down their half-conscious defenses. He stripped from them their self-conceit. He unveiled the hidden plague of their hearts.

He made it plain to Nicodemus that, *as he was,* teacher of Israel and all, so far from entering into the Kingdom of God, he could not even see it (John 3:5).

He got beneath the Samaritan woman's cynical indifference, so that she broadcast to all who would hear, "He told me all things that ever I did" (John 4:29).

Simon Peter was the boaster among the disciples. There were times when he would have been much better off if he had kept his mouth shut. But there came a day when he faced the Truth, and the only thing he could say was, "Depart from me, for I am a sinful man, O Lord" (Luke 5:8).

In each case, the vision of Truth brought with it the offer of Grace. Nicodemus came to see that a New Birth was not only necessary, but gloriously possible. The Samaritan woman who began with a sneer ended with an earnest prayer, because she saw there were living waters available to her. Peter's request was not granted, because he did not mean what he said. He spoke in the heat and confusion of surging emotion. When he became rational again, he saw that he was being offered fellowship with the One who could change him from what he actually was to what he ought to be. Jesus came to each one of them "full of grace and truth."

As the Truth, He is the full and perfect Revelation. As Grace, He is the Author of perfect Redemption. He not only diagnoses the trouble, but He also prescribes and offers the perfect remedy.

* * * * *

Each year, when we come round to the marvelous Advent

Season, we should try to get a new slant on it. As faithful Pastor Robinson said of old, "God hath yet more light and truth to break forth from His Holy Word." Have we ever tried to relate the message of Christmas to that great pronouncement, "Jesus Christ is the same, yesterday, and today, and for ever" (Hebrews 13:8)?

If we will try to do this, we shall come to see that in the midst of our needy twentieth century we can find in Him the very thing people found two thousand years ago.

Sing we then in Jesu's name,
Now as yesterday the same;
One in every time and place,
Full, for all, of truth and grace.

—Charles Wesley

His light can still shine into the darkest corners of our hearts, revealing the unpleasant truth about ourselves. We need no longer have false opinions about ourselves. We need not despair either, for it is still true that *with the Truth there comes the Grace.*

If we see the Truth that comes in Him alone, we shall also see the Grace that comes in Him alone, for this, too, is part of the Truth. He comes *to us* "full of grace,"

Grace to cover all my sin,

not in the sense of hiding it either from God's sight or my own, but in the sense of "blotting it out."

This is "the Grace of our Lord Jesus Christ." It is "Love to the loveless shown," not that they might still be loved in spite of their unlovableness, but that Holy Love might transform them, "that they might lovely be."

We are without hope in this world if we are without God (Ephesians 2:12). But there is no reason why we should be either, "For God so loved the world, that he gave his only begotten Son, that whosoever believeth in him should not perish, but have everlasting life" (John 3:16).

He came "full of grace and truth" . . . .
Truth that condemns. . . . Grace that saves. . . .
Truth that hurts. . . . Grace that heals. . . .
Truth that puts to death the old life of self and sin. . . .
Grace that brings to birth within the heart Christ's new life of humble trust and loving obedience. . . .

A Saviour born, in love supreme,
He comes our fallen souls to raise;
He comes His people to redeem
With all His plenitude of Grace.

—Charles Wesley

7

The Name Which Is Above Every Name

WE DO NOT ATTACH MUCH IMPORTANCE TO NAMES. THEY have no special meaning for us. They identify us, but they do not describe us. We can know the name of a person without having the slightest idea what he is like.

The Hebrews believed the name was an integral part of the personality. It was the embodiment of the character. If you knew someone's name, you knew what kind of a man he was. The name *Jacob* (Genesis 27:36) indicated that he was a wily supplanter who could not be trusted. *Barak* (Judges 4:6) means "lightning." He was the kind of man who could strike anywhere without warning. *Caleb* (Numbers 13:6) was a "dog" to be despised. *Deborah* (Genesis 35:8; Judges 4:4) means "bee." She could be as sweet as honey, but she never lost her sting. *Huldah* (2 Kings 22:14) was a "weasel."

Similarly, the name of a place often indicated its outstanding feature. *Carmel* (Joshua 15:55) was a "garden land." *Ekron* (Amos 1:8) was "barren." *Gibeah* (Hosea 5:8) was a "hill." *Horeb* was "dry." If you knew the names of these places you had a pretty good idea what to expect when you got there.

The Name Which Is Above Every Name

The Hebrews had many names for God. Each one describes some truth about Him, or His ways, or His purposes for men. *El* is an ancient and widespread Semitic name for God. Although the root meaning of the word seems to be *power,* primitive people did not think in abstract terms, and for them it probably meant "the strong One," "the powerful One." *Elohim* is a plural form. It is not the plural of *El*, which is *Elim.* In modern times we have become accustomed to the regal use of "we." Queen Victoria inadvertently witnessed a satire of herself and haughtily stalked out of the room, commenting, "We are not amused." This usage may be a very old custom. *Elohim* may be the plural of "majesty," indicating "the Sovereign One." *El Shaddai* means "God the Almighty." *Jehovah* is an English word which cannot be traced further back than the Reformation. It is a hybrid. The consonants of one Hebrew word were mistakenly wedded to the vowels of another. The Hebrew word is *Yahweh.* Originally, it seems to have meant "I will be." It is easy to see how that would become "He will be," implying "He will be all that we can ever need."

The Jews identified the name with the person. In their devout and deep reverence for God, they often preferred to speak of "the name of God" when what they actually meant was "God." I understand that at camp meetings and places where believers shout, enthusiastic worshippers are sometimes heard to exclaim, "Praise His Name!" What they mean, of course, is "Praise Him." This is quite acceptable Hebrew. It is found all through the Old Testament.

"The name of the God of Jacob defend thee" (Psalm 20:1) either means "The God of Jacob defend thee," or we are moving in the realm of magic. "Let them that love thy name be joyful in thee" (Psalm 5:11) must mean "Let them that love *thee* be joyful in thee." In Hebrew poetry, the second line of a couplet repeats the thought of the previous line in slightly different words. So, in

I will praise the Lord according to his righteousness;
And will sing praise to the name of the Lord most high (Psalm 7:17),

"the name of the Lord" in the second line parallels "the Lord" in the first line.

The Jews were fond of using the expression "the name of God" to denote all they knew about Him. It was their responsibility to "declare his name" (Exodus 9:16; 22:22; etc.), i.e. *what He was to them,* to the ends of the earth. Similarly, when the Chosen People were said to "know the name" of God, it meant to know *Him,* to know *what He is like.* God is said to act "for his name's sake" (Ezekiel 20:9; etc.). This implies that He does not belie Himself. He acts in complete harmony with His character so far as it has been revealed to His people.

* * * * *

The Old Testament cry was, "Oh, that I knew where I might find him!" (Job 23:3). The spirit of man could not define the object of its desire. It was certain, however, that there must be Something, or Someone, that could satisfy its deepest longings.

The Prophets were restless. The Seers of old were forever groping. Age after age, they hopefully proclaimed, "He that shall come, will come, and not tarry" (Habakkuk 2:3).

At last this Joy of man's desiring appears on earth. In His coming He quickens the quest. As a Babe in Bethlehem, seemingly so weak and helpless, He attracts the Wise Men from the distant East, and the humble Shepherds from the nearby fields.

Jesus is God's final answer to man's petition, "Tell me, I pray thee, thy name" (Genesis 32:29). "Thou shalt call his name *Jesus*" (Matthew 1:21; Luke 1:31).

The Jews seem to have had no definite rule as to who should name a child. Often the mother chose the name (Genesis 4:25; 16:11; 19:37ff.; Judges 13:23; 1 Samuel 1:20; etc.), but there are almost as many instances of the name being given by the father (Genesis 5:3; 16:15; 17:19; Isaiah 8:1, 3; Hosea 1:4; etc.).

Neither Mary nor Joseph chose the name of the Babe. It was decided before He was born. It was determined in the councils of heaven. Lest there should be any doubt about it, it was revealed to Joseph as well as to Mary. At the Annunciation, the angel Gabriel said to the Virgin, "Fear not, Mary; for thou hast found favor with God. And, behold, thou shalt conceive in thy womb, and bring forth a son, and shalt call his name Jesus" (Luke 1:30f.). When an angel of the Lord prepared Joseph for this strange turn of events, he gave him the explicit command, "Thou shalt call his name Jesus" (Matthew 1:21).

Jesus is the Greek rendering of a sacred and heroic name in Israel. It is frequently found in the Old Testament. It appears in such various forms as *Oshea* (Numbers 13:8), *Hoshea* (Deuteronomy 32:44), *Heshua* (1 Chronicles 24:11), *Jehoshua* (Numbers 13:16), *Jeshua* (Ezra 2:2), and *Joshua*.

The most famous bearer of this noble name was "Joshua the son of Nun, Moses' minister" (Joshua 1:1), who led the Chosen People into the Promised Land, after the death of Moses. It was he who gave his name to the sixth book in the Bible.

This great name was borne by the heroic high priest who returned from the Exile with Zerubbabel, aided him in the restoration of the Temple, and proved to be such an encourager of the people (Haggai 1:1, 12, 14; Ezra 3:7, 9).

It was also the name of that godly and winsome Jerusalemite, Jesus the son of Sirach. Nearly two hundred years before the Advent of the Messiah, he wrote the lovely book of Ecclesiasticus. Perhaps the best known of his proverbs is, "He that toucheth pitch shall be defiled" (13:1), while his most familiar passage is that choice canticle which begins with the mis-translation, "Now praise we great and famous men."

The root meaning of the name *Jesus* is "Jehovah is Salvation" or, "God our Saviour." During the hectic days of the Maccabean insurrection, the name *Jesus* served as a battle-cry.

In the New Testament there are four others who bore this name besides the Son of Mary. When Paul and Barnabas visited Paphos, on their First Missionary Journey, their work was hindered by a magician named *Bar-Jesus,* who evidently exerted considerable influence over the pro-consul (Acts 13:6). Paul speaks highly of the faithful service rendered to him by "Jesus, which is called Justus" (Colossians 4:11). In the genealogy of our Lord given in the Third Gospel, reference is made to "Er, the son of Jesus" (Luke 3:28f.).

In some of the older versions of the New Testament, the full name of the malefactor whom Pilate offered to the people is given as "Jesus Barabbas." Moffatt's translation, the Revised Standard Version (margin), and the brilliant New English Bible accept this text. If, as seems probable, this is correct, then what the governor actually said to the people was, "Whom will ye that I release unto you, Jesus Barabbas [i.e., Jesus-the-son-of-the-father], or Jesus which is called Christ [i.e., Jesus which is called *the Anointed*]?" (Matthew 27:17). In other words, the cynical Pilate sought to heighten the drama by asking them which *Jesus* they preferred. Was the Salvation of Jehovah to be found in a seditionist or a martyr?

The translators of the King James Version erred without reason when they gave *Jesus* for *Joshua* in Hebrews 4:8.

* * * * *

Paul says *Jesus* is the "name which is above every name" (Philippians 2:9).

The Name Which Is Above Every Name

In "The Golden Legend," Longfellow tells how, in the writing-room of an ancient monastery, Friar Pacificus laid down his pen with the words,

It is growing dark! Yet one line more
And then my work for to-day is o'er.
I come again to the name of the Lord!
Ere I that awful name record,
That is spoken so lightly among men,
Let me pause awhile, and wash my pen;
Pure from blemish and blot must it be,
When it writes that word of mystery.

"The name which is above every name!" Yet when Paul penned these magnificent words, the name of Jesus was unknown to all but a few thousand people. To most of them it was merely the name of a dead Jew. Today, the name of Jesus is high above every name.

Jesus! the name high over all,
In hell, or earth, or sky;
Angels and men before it fall,
And devils fear and fly.

—Charles Wesley

There is no name in the world so widely known and honored. There is no name so often remembered and so greatly loved. There is no name more precious to young and old alike. It is cherished by millions whose careers are opening out before them. It means even more to those whose course is run.

Through Him the first fond prayers are said
Our lips of childhood frame,
The last low whispers of our dead
Are burdened with His name.

—John Greenleaf Whittier

What makes the name appropriate for the Virgin's Son is its prophetic significance. "Thou shalt call his name Jesus; for *he shall save his people from their sins*" (Matthew 1:21).

This prediction soars beyond natural aspiration. It does not indicate political power. It does not speak of military triumphs. It does not promise material success. It does not forecast universal fame.

The prophecy is moral and spiritual. It is higher than national sovereignty. It is wider, even, than global supremacy. It was never claimed for any other child than the Christ-Child, "for there is none other name under heaven, given among men, whereby we must be saved" (Acts 4:12).

The angel said to the Shepherds, "Unto you is born this day in the city of David a Saviour, which is Christ the Lord" (Luke 2:11). This is the first occurrence of the word "Saviour" in the New Testament. It is its solitary appearance in Luke's gospel. Matthew and Mark never use it. It occurs only once in the Fourth Gospel, and then it is found on the lips of a Samaritan! (John 4:42).

"Christ the Lord" is not found anywhere else in the whole of the New Testament.

Yet these titles have become exceedingly precious to the Universal Church, as signifying the redemptive ministry for which, when the fullness of the time was come, Jesus entered the world.

Paul was a great phrase-maker. He put the meaning of Jesus in graphic and forcible words. If Paul has said it, it does not need to be said again. In Galatians 4:4, he has the right phrase for the Christian conviction that Jesus did not just happen to be born where He was and when He was. Arguing that the Jewish Law must give place to the Christian Revelation, Paul declares that it was in *the fulness of the time* that God sent forth His Son.

In his delightful book, *People's Life of Christ,* Professor

Paterson Smythe gives a full and suggestive answer to the question, What are we to understand by "the fulness of the time"? He shows the preparation of the centuries for the coming of Jesus "to save his people from their sins."

The Hebrew people were unique in their worship of one God. The Greeks fashioned the most perfect tongue the world had ever known. The Romans built the roads which connected the whole world, and made them safe for travelers.

Judaism was the mould which held the Good News. *The Greek language* was the vehicle to carry the Good News. *The Roman Empire* was ready to spread the Good News.

Jesus came at the right time. He came to a world of failure. At the end of their centuries of probation, the Jews were both an unsatisfied and an unsatisfactory people. The glory of Greece was a thing of the past. Roman rule was cruel and tyrannical. It was an unhappy, suspicious, fearful, needy world.

Jesus came to a world of despair. Plutarch tells of a ship, bound for Italy, laden with merchandise and passengers, which was becalmed one evening "off the Isles Echinades." As they drifted by Paxos, a voice was heard from the island calling, "Thamus." Thamus, who was the Egyptian pilot, ignored the first two calls, but answered the third. Then this message came to him, "When you come over against Palodes, announce that the Great Pan is dead." Thamus did not know what to do, so he decided that if there was a good breeze he would sail by Palodes as if nothing had happened, but if there was a calm, he would proclaim what he had heard. When they reached the appointed place there was neither wind nor wave, and Thamus, looking from the bow of the boat to the land, cried, "The Great Pan is dead!" Immediately there arose the wail of the mourning of multitudes. Such stories, and they are many, show what despair had filled men's hearts when Jesus came.

Yet it was a world of religion. Much of the religion was ignoble, but the people of the first century were feeling after

God as perhaps never before and never since. Everywhere the blind forces of life were groping and crying underfoot. It was a world of expectancy. It was, indeed, "the fulness of the time." The preparations were complete. The conditions were ripe for Him to appear "to save his people from their sins."

* * * * *

The New Testament looks at "Salvation" from three angles at least. This does not mean there are three or more theories competing for first place. Rather, it means that while all the writers look at the subject from varying points of view, each emphasizes the one which best suits his immediate purpose. There is, therefore, both an overlapping and an interlocking. In our feverish desire to separate "The Gospel according to Paul" from "The Gospel according to Peter," we have often forgotten this important consideration.

From John's standpoint, Salvation is *knowledge* of God, "This is life eternal, to know thee, the only true God" (John 17:3). Paul, however, saturates his writings with a great emphasis upon *deliverance*. Salvation is deliverance from the pain, penalty, and power of sin (cf. Romans 6; Galatians 1:4; 1 Thessalonians 1:10; etc.).

Let us see first what Jesus has to say about this.

He knew, better than anyone else, what human life might be. He knew that God intended it to be happy, holy, healthy, and free. Yet everywhere He went, He saw people miserable, sinful, ill, and in bondage to fear. He sought to save them from everything that spoiled their lives.

Do you remember how Jesus spoke about people whom we call wicked and bad? He said they were lost, and He had come to find them (Matthew 18:12; Luke 19:10; etc.). He said they were sick, and He had come to heal them (Matthew 9:12; Mark 2:17; etc.).

Jesus did not judge people. He did not punish them. He did

not send them to prison. "I came not to judge the world," He said (John 12:47), but "to seek and to save that which was lost" (Luke 19:10).

It is a very arresting thing that while Jesus sometimes talked to good people about badness, He always talked to bad people about goodness. He did not say, "You are bad people, and if you do not mend your ways, God will punish you." He did not even promise bad people that if they were good they would go to heaven when they died.

He made friends with them. He showed them by His own life and words and deeds how beautiful goodness was. He taught them they were God's children (Matthew 6:4, 6; etc.). He said they must be like their Father in heaven (Matthew 5:45, 48; etc.).

How could they be like their Father in heaven unless they knew Him?

* * * * *

John says that no one but Jesus can give the knowledge of God, because He is "the only begotten of the Father" (John 1:14). "No man hath seen God at any time; the only begotten Son, which is in the bosom of the Father, he hath declared him" (John 1:18). It was Jesus' own contention that "he that hath seen me hath seen the Father" (John 14:9). Jesus is God's Representative to us.

The modern commercial world is well acquainted with the duly appointed representative, the one who has the ability and the authority to tell you anything you want to know about his firm or its products.

Jesus has the ability and the authority to tell us about God. More than this, *He came to show us God.* When we look at Jesus, we say with Goethe, "The Divine can never be more divine than that." The great body of the Christian Church holds a positive doctrine concerning the Person of Christ, namely, that He was the eternal Son of God, who, for our sakes, became Man. The Christian Church believes that He was God as well as Man. It has always believed this, though it has not always expressed itself succinctly. We must, consequently, be careful to abandon and reject those statements of the doctrine of Christ's Person which ultimately present us with a schizophrenic. The familiar formulation of "Two Natures in One Person" raises more problems than it solves. "The formula of two natures in one person does not adequately reproduce the impression that He makes. He is all one — that is the very strongest conviction we have. . . . All that is Divine in Him is human, all that is human is Divine. He is not separately, or even distinctly, Son of God and Son of Man, but the Son of Man who is the Son of God."[1]

There are many people in our world who know little of God. A lot of them would like to know more about Him. Somehow, they have never met His Representative.

For long centuries, men lived in darkness, groping after the truth about God. They stumbled nearer and nearer. They were never able to establish full contact. Then Jesus came.

Tennyson's great poem *In Memoriam* contains a beautiful ode which suggests a reason for the Incarnation.

For Wisdom dealt with mortal powers,
Where truth in closest words shall fail,
When truth embodied in a tale
Shall enter in at lowly doors.

Divine truth could not be brought home to men in close philosophical argument. It best enters "lowly doors" by earthly similitudes and parables. What a word is to thought, Christ is to God. He is the Divine Articulation.

[1] James Denny, *Studies in Theology,* pp. 68f.

And so the Word had breath, and wrought
With human hands the creed of creeds
In loveliness of perfect deeds,
More strong than all poetic thought.

The coming of Christ was the coming of God. By looking at Jesus we discover what God is like. In Him we see the Father's love perfectly revealed. He displays the Father's concern, the Father's heart. He shows what God thinks about us.

The English actor Forbes-Robertson relates that in his London Club there was an atheist by the name of Crowe. In season and out of season, he preached his unbelief. He never missed an opportunity to attack Christianity. Finally, one of the members whote on the Club bulletin board,

We've heard in language highly spiced
That Crowe does not believe in Christ.
But what we're more concerned to know
Is whether Christ believes in Crowe.

John does not hesitate to supply the answer. He says that Jesus is God taking the trouble to seek us out wherever we may be, because we do not have even the inclination to seek Him out. Though we deserve condemnation, Jesus did not come "to condemn the world, but that the world through Him might be saved" (John 3:17).

Whenever the Fourth Evangelist uses the designation "the world," it always has the sinister connotation of "the world organized against God," "the rebellious world." We cannot spare time for Him, but He loves us. We fail to take Him seriously, but the Word became flesh and dwelt among us. We forget Him as soon as we get outside the church door, but He has promised to be with us always.

A little girl awoke one night, and cried because she was afraid of the dark. Her mother tried to comfort her by saying, "You mustn't be afraid of the dark. God is always near you." Her troubled daughter replied, "Yes, I know that. . . . But I'd rather He had a face." God has a face. "He that hath seen me hath seen the Father." We call the face of God "Jesus." He is God's unveiling of *Himself* to this world.

When we see Him, we not only know what God is like, we also know what God wants us to be. The noblest adjective in our language is not the word *Godlike,* wonderful as that may be. The noblest adjective is the word *Christlike.* That is what God wants us to be.

Somehow, the knowledge of God has transforming power. When we see Perfect Goodness personified in Him whose Name is above every name, we are "transformed into the same image from glory to glory" (2 Corinthians 3:18), and our Salvation has begun.

* * * * *

Paul says everything that John says, and sometimes he says it better. It is his superb prose that speaks of seeing "the light of the knowledge of the glory of God in the face of Jesus Christ" (2 Corinthians 4:6).

Salvation, says Paul, is deliverance from sin (Romans 7:24f.). One of his massive words is *liberty.* He speaks of "the glorious liberty of the children of God" (Romans 8:21). He insists that "where the Spirit of the Lord is, there is liberty" (2 Corinthians 3:17). He bids his converts "stand fast in the liberty wherewith Christ made us free" (Galatians 5:1).

This deliverance is the work of Christ, but it is based upon the Person of Christ. With John, Paul recognizes that this is the all-important factor in Salvation. What Jesus does depends upon who He is. Humanity cannot of itself produce its own Redeemer. Jesus is the Son of God. He is "the image of the invisible God" (Colossians 1:15). He is "the Son of God, who loved me, and gave himself for me" (Galatians 2:

20). "God was in Christ reconciling the world unto himself" (2 Corinthians 5:19) — *doing what God alone could do.* Only *God* can "save his people from their sins."

Canon Liddon once reminded us that Plato is not Platonism. Platonism might have been developed by a school of thinkers. It could have evolved even if Plato had never lived. Similarly, Mohammed is not Islam. The Koran brands as unpardonable idolatry any attempt to identify its religion with the Prophet. *But Christ Himself is Christianity.* His teaching has value because *He* uttered it. It is "through him" that we "have access to the Father" (Ephesians 2:18). It is not through His teaching, not even through His deeds, but "through him." It is because of what He *is* that we can come to the Father through Him.

This is what the New Testament means when it speaks of believing in "the name of Jesus." To believe in the Name of Jesus is to believe in Jesus. The Name indicates the Personality. It is surely significant that the writer who refers most frequently to "the name of Jesus" alternates such references with the phrase "to believe in Jesus" (cf. John 1:12; 2:23; 3:16, 18; 6:40). "The name of Jesus" is a parallel term to the word "Jesus" itself. It is appropriately used because "the name of Jesus" sums up the personality of Jesus as made known to men. To believe "in his name" is to believe in Him, and accept His claims.

It stands written, "No man cometh to the Father, but by me" (John 14:6).

None other Lamb, none other Name,
None other hope in heaven or earth or sea,
None other hiding-place from guilt and shame,
None beside Thee.

—Christina Georgina Rossetti

Wherefore God also hath highly exalted him, and given him a name which is above every name; that at the name of Jesus every knee should bow, of things in heaven, and things in earth, and things under the earth; and that every tongue should confess that Jesus Christ is Lord, to the glory of God the Father (Philippians 2:9f.).

8

The Source of Life

In him was life (John 1:4).

THERE ARE TWO GREEK WORDS FOR "LIFE." WE HAVE borrowed both of them, and they occur in quite ordinary English words. When the Greeks wanted to describe life, they used the word *bios,* from which we get such words as *bio*graphy, *bio*logy, *bio*chemistry, *bio*psy, *bio*tics, and the like. The other Greek word is *zoē,* from which we get words like *zo*ology, *zo*otic, *zo*odynamics, etc. *Zoē* means "the essence of life."

Zoē is the term used by the Fourth Evangelist is his magnificent Prologue. We should not go far wrong if we translated this statement: "In Him was the essence of life."

The one thing which baffles everyone, the one secret which puzzles all scientists, the one element which no laboratory has yet produced, the mystery of mysteries, "the essence of life" — was "in him."

It is "the essence of life" which makes all the difference. If it isn't in a grain of corn, there is no use sowing that grain. If it isn't in an egg, that egg will never hatch. If it isn't in the tiny cells from which human beings spring, no new person will come to bless and enrich the home.

Anyone who says that man is not clever merely reveals himself to be a fool. Man has split the atom, launched the satellites, and even learned how to harness the energy of the distant sun. But — and it is a tremendous "but" — man does not know what life in its essence is. It still staggers not only his thought, but his imagination as well. All man's theories about "the essence of life" make little more sense than Haeckel's unreasonable and easily disproved doctrine of "Spontaneous Generation," or that other absurdity which he borrowed from Lucretius, "The Fortuitous Concourse of Atoms."

Unless we are prepared to say, humbly and reverently, scarcely knowing what we mean, "In the beginning was the Word. . . . In him was the essence of life," we have no satisfactory explanation to the mystery of existence. The only answer came on that first Christmas: "The Word became flesh" (John 1:14).

* * * * *

Jesus Christ, the Son of God and the Son of Mary, assured those ancient mourners, "I am the resurrection and the life" (John 11:25). When Thomas, in his great perplexity and anxiety, confessed his ignorance to his Master, Jesus replied, "I am the way, the truth, and the life" (John 14:6). When the Jews harassed Jesus in the Temple, He said to them, "As the Father hath life in himself, so hath he given to the Son to have life in himself" (John 5:26). This is the Son who "quickeneth whom he will" (John 5:21). One of the majestic claims of Jesus is enshrined in the familiar words, "I am come that they might have life, and that they might have it more abundantly" (John 10:10).

"I am come. . . ." The message of Christmas is that *something happened.* The Apostles were quite definite about it.

"The Word became flesh, and dwelt among us" (John 1:14). "When the fulness of the time was come, God sent forth his Son" (Galatians 4:4). Peter insists that Jesus Christ, "who was foreknown indeed before the foundation of the world . . . was manifest at the end of the times for your sake" (1 Peter 1:20). The author of the Epistle to the Hebrews bases all his arguments on the fact that "God, who at sundry times and in divers manners spake in time past unto the fathers through the prophets, hath in these last days spoken unto us in his Son" (Hebrew 1:1f.).

When John came to write his First Epistle, he could find no better beginning than to re-emphasize the facts of his own experience. "That . . . which we have heard, that which we have seen with our eyes, that which we have looked upon, and our hands have handled of the Word of life: for the life was manifested, and we have seen it, and bear witness, and shew unto you that eternal life, which was with the Father, and was manifested unto us; that which we have seen and heard declare we unto you" (1 John 1:1ff.).

Here on this solid earth of ours a decisive, historic event once took place. It was something in flesh and blood which men saw and heard for themselves. It was something which so affected them that they wrote it into the record, "The Word became flesh."

Christianity has a concrete, historic context. It did not begin as a myth, a fancy, or a cunningly devised fable. "In the days of Herod the king . . . Jesus was born in Bethlehem of Judea" (Matthew 2:1).

Jesus Christ is a fact of human experience. He made His own impression upon men and women. They came under His spell. They felt His transforming power. They understood that He had come for a *purpose*.

* * * * *

The message of Christmas is that Jesus came to make all life divine. He came to bring us into such conscious nearness to God, into such vital fellowship with Him, that we should be able to discern God's will in this world, and to link our wills with His in a perpetual consecration that makes sense of life.

Life without God is life without pattern.

Perhaps you are old enough to remember the kaleidoscope. It was a cylinder full of odds and ends which seemed to have no relation to one another, until you looked at them through the eye-piece. When you did this, a pattern immediately became apparent. You saw beautiful colors and symmetrical forms. Actually, nothing had happened to the odds and ends, but because you looked at them in the right way a meaningful pattern appeared.

The manifold situations of life are not necessarily altered, whether we view them through the eye-piece or not. However, when we do look at them in the right way, we see that they hold together. Jesus came to show us how to look at life.

The measure of the world is not the measure of eternity. Because of the limits of their restricted vision, our modern world seems to be a hodge-podge of unrelated problems to many people.

If scientists and politicians the world over came to look upon the discoveries in nuclear physics through the eye-piece provided by God, a pattern would be discerned.

Paul evidently faced this kind of situation. He found it necessary to write, "Eye hath not seen, nor ear heard, neither have entered into the heart of man, the things which God hath prepared for them that love him. But God hath revealed them unto us by his Spirit: for the Spirit searcheth all things, yea, the deep things of God" (1 Corinthians 2:9f.).

The ministry of Jesus seems to be a series of unrelated items and situations. The people with whom He had to do were a motley crowd. There were farmers, fishermen, merchants, tax-gatherers, soldiers, and folks of varying national strands.

They were as incongruous a group as you could find in a day's march through New York City. Yet because He viewed them all from the standpoint of love, they all became related, and each had his place.

Jesus came into contact with pain, joy, sorrow, revelings, bereavement and disappointment. Because He viewed them all in the light of redemptive love, wherever He went He could say, "This day is salvation come to this house" (Luke 19:9).

These memorable words were actually spoken in the home of a very rich man. That fact, however, was entirely incidental. In this case, the "salvation" was, from the material point of view, an extremely costly thing. It often is.

When Jesus said He came to bestow more abundant life, He was not thinking of giving us additional items. Perhaps most of us are already overloaded with life's impedimenta. Yet the urge of the age is to *get*. Very few people live at the present. They are "getting" for the future. Today is not theirs. They are looking forward to an indefinite tomorrow when they will "have enough." Then, they say, they will live. Their whole conception of life is tied up with *things*. They toil for the meat which perishes. They achieve worldly wealth, but at the same time, heavenly poverty. They couple economic stability with emotional instability. They have bodily fullness and soul frustration. They experience material satiety and spiritual starvation. They know the price of everything and the value of nothing. They are being forced to learn afresh, in a hard school, the truth of the Master's words, "What shall it profit a man, if he shall gain the whole world, and lose his own soul?" (Mark 8:36).

When Jesus spoke of giving "abundant life," He was thinking, not of material possessions, but, rather, of the approach to life. He offers us the ability to see life as He sees it. It is this perspective which gives His people an opposite set of values from the world. In a world that says, "Matter," the

Church says, "Spirit." To a world that says "Man," the Church says, "God." In a society that says, "Get," the Church counsels, "Give." To an age that has deified "Lust," the Church offers "Love." When people say, "Find life," the Church says, "Lose life." To an existential philosophy that knows only "Now," the Church speaks of "Eternity." To those who cry, "Master," the Church answers, "Serve." To those who preach, "Conquer," the Church says, "Redeem." Where the world speaks of an "Alien," the Church speaks of a "Brother." When the world says, "Enemy," the Church says, "Friend." The world is concerned with what *I* want, the Church with what *God* wants.

Our fellow-being becomes an entirely new creature when we see he is a person for whom Christ lived and died. And not only is a new dimension given to others, but our own life becomes more abundant as we reflect upon the glorious significance of human creation.

God created us in His own likeness. That means He created us for fellowship with Himself. The Old Testament tells us as much as this. Christmas tells us a great deal more. We are not sufficient unto ourselves. We are not equipped for independence.

Back in the morning of the wistful years
God dreamed a wonder-dream, and then He spake:
"Lo, out of dust a mystery will I make:
Make man, and dower him with the gift of tears,
With dreams and valors, and the shadow fears,
With love and longing and a heart to break,
A free soul poised for mastery or mistake, —
Then leave him alone before the great careers!
I know the risk, the terror of my deed,
Yet I must make him free to be the seed
Of seraphim who guard the cosmic gates:

Behold in his hand the glory and the curse
As he goes forth to build eternal fates:
Now there is danger in the Universe!"
—Edwin Markham

We ourselves are not the masters of life until we acknowledge and confess Him as our Master. Although Jesus promised abundant life to those who come to Him, He also made it plain that only those who are prepared to lose their lives can come to Him, but they are to lose them, as He said, "for my sake and the gospel's" (Mark 8:34).

Once from the boat He taught the curious throng,
Then bade me cast my net into the sea;
I murmured but obeyed, nor was it long
Before the catch amazed and humbled me.
His was the boat, And His the skill,
And His the catch, And His my will.
—George Macdonald

Life needs an *aim,* if it is to be completely satisfying. Secondary, selfish aims just will not do, for to live without an all-engaging, worthy ambition soon leads to futility, frustration, and despair. *Ours is a frustrated age, not because people can't get what they want, but because what they want is not worth having.*

A great and absorbing passion gives meaning and enthusiasm and satisfaction to all our labors. Bernard Newman told how the peasant daughter of a house he visited in the Balkans spent all her time sewing. He thought she must be sewing to make a living. "Don't you ever get tired, stitch, stitch, stitching away?" he asked. "Oh, no, sir," she said, "You see, this is my wedding-dress."

* * * * *

The message of Christmas is not only that God has a purpose. Jesus came that everyone may find a place in this purpose. We may direct all our activities to God's purpose for us and for the world. When we do this, we find the secret of the life which is abundant.

Everyone can co-operate in God's eternal purpose. No one can frustrate it. The Bible states very clearly that God's Sovereignty does not depend on our response. God is still Sovereign even when we ignore His purpose or defy His call. Man's freedom in no way limits God's Lordship. He can make even "the wrath of men" to praise Him (Psalm 76:10). God neither condones wickedness nor endorses indifference. He overrides these things, so that the end is His, not man's. The vilest, most rebellious thing men ever did was to crucify the Son of God. Yet today millions sing, "In the Cross of Christ I Glory."

To those who would learn from Him the secret of abundant life, Jesus gives the ability to assess life's varied experiences. It is here that we so often fail. We do not know what to do with our experiences.

Experience has the power either to enrich or to degrade our character. It all depends on how we react to experience, on what we allow it to do to us and for us. I think it was Dr. Fosdick who once said, "Circumstances only pull the trigger. What happens depends upon what is in the man to explode."

In other words, experience is very largely what we make of it. Christmas tells us there is something precious in everything that happens to us, because God is there to meet us in all the experiences through which we are called upon to pass. This is the message of Christmas which we call "Emmanuel, God with us." It assures us that we do not walk alone, because "something happened" that first Christmas — "the Word," in whom was Life, "became flesh and dwelt among us."

Let praise devote thy work and skill employ
Thy whole mind, and thy heart be lost in joy.
Well-doing bringeth pride, this constant thought
Humility, that thy best done is naught.
Man doeth nothing well, be it great or small,
Save to praise God; but that hath saved all:
For God requires no more than thou hast done,
And takes thy work to bless it for His own.

—Robert Bridges

* * * * *

But the message of Christmas has more to say to us. It not only says, "Something happened," but also, "Something *can* happen." It says that Jesus is here, in this twentieth century. He is in our churches, in our homes, and in our daily work. Because of this, something *can* happen, to us, today. Something can happen *because Jesus is here.*

Jesus is not to be limited to His own age, country, and race. He belongs to all time, and to every land and people. The historic event that took place nearly two thousand years ago has a vital significance for every generation, including ours. "Jesus Christ is the same, yesterday and today and for ever" (Hebrews 13:8).

Perhaps we realize that to a small degree. We would not attend the house of worship but for the knowledge that "wherever two or three are gathered together in my name, there am I in the midst of them" (Matthew 18:20).

We also feel that at least the influence of Christ must be in our modern world if we, and millions upon millions like us everywhere, are preparing to celebrate again the wonder of His birth. That, of course, is something. No one else in history is honored so universally, so long after his time. In that sense, Jesus "is here" for us.

We may realize that Jesus is present today, still influencing us in the laws that His teaching and His Spirit have caused to be written in this nation's statute books. In that sense "He is here."

Or He may "be here" for us in our own highest ideals and standards, ideals and standards which we have inherited from an environment permeated by His Spirit. When we think about this, we are sometimes thrown into doubt. We wonder if there is as much of the Spirit of Christ in our environment as we like to imagine. The ban on prayer in public schools, and the incredible endorsement of this outrage by church leaders, ought to have shaken us out of our lethargy. Instead, it seemed to stun us. We are now being told not to bring religion into government. And what about the press? The small-town newspapers still do a good job of religious reporting. But the metropolitan press? Its policy seems to be: Give the latest news of murders. Placard on the front page the latest husband of the much-divorced film star. Scream of scandal in high places, especially if commercialized sex can be introduced. But the foundation-stone on which the whole of our Western culture is built — Christ and His religion? Keep that for the back page where it will attract least attention, and cut it as required. Over against this, however, the astounding fact remains that the world's "best seller" continues to be the Bible. So long as that influences our ideals and standards, we can say that "Christ is here" in them.

Or we may be aware of His presence in our conscience, that troublesome thing within us which, because of Christ, we have to deal with, one way or another. D. L. Moody once said, "I have great respect for the woman that started out during the war with a poker. She heard the enemy were coming and went to resist them. When someone asked her what she could do with a poker, she said she would at least let them know what side she was on." When we are obedient to conscience so that people know what side we are on, "Christ is here."

In all these ways we may think of Christ as "here." But they are not enough. As the Church has proclaimed since its earliest days, the purpose of Christ's birth in Bethlehem was that He might be born in each human heart. The assurance of the Christian is expressed in the testimony of Paul, "Christ liveth in me" (Galatians 2:20). This is the source of the abundant life.

We live by things too vast for human thought, as we live by thoughts too deep for human tears. We live by the fullness of the life of God, which we but see and know in scattered rays now, but in whose full glory we shall all be bathed when the morning stars sing together, and all the sons of God shout for joy, as the day breaks and the shadows flee away.

9

The Light of Men

JESUS CAME TO SHOW US LIFE AS IT OUGHT TO BE. "IN HIM was life, and the life was the light of men" (John 1:4).

All illumination aims at transforming the actual into the possible. Men filled with the Spirit of God will neither suspect every new voice nor allow themselves to be captives to what was said by them of old time.

Yet new knowledge often comes more as a blow to pride than as a shaft of light to the mind. It is the natural tendency of all of us to resist new ideas when to accept them means a painful readjustment on our part. It is bad enough when we are fearful of having our shallow orthodoxy ruffled. It is worse when we identify prejudice with principle.

We live in a totem-ridden society, full of fear. The great fear is the fear of change. That is perhaps the reason so many people fear the views of those they secretly despise. All newness is at first uncouth, but that hardly justifies the attitude of those who would rather live for prestige than die for conviction.

The truth is, we are quite comfortable as we are. We are

fully satisfied with our present condition. No one can deny that our way of life works very well for us and for most people we know. We do not have a tremendous interest in those we do not know. We object to talking about "transforming the actual into the possible," when the actual itself suits us so well. And so we close our eyes to the "illumination." Or, rather, we close our minds. We invent labels of an uncomplimentary nature to stick on those who would disturb our cherished lethargy. We maintain our sweet selfish smiles in the presence of those who ask unnecessary or embarrassing questions, but we do not listen to them. We regard such people as suspicious characters. They have no place in a society which identifies existence with its own culture. We avoid them as people shun a creditor whom they cannot pay.

We are content with our lot because we dwell in the gloom. Now we see through a glass darkly. We have a small grasp of the meaning of life. Yet God's people must never worship at the pagan shrine of "as is."

Our understanding of the meaning of life depends on three related factors. First, the range and depth of our own personal experience. Second, our ability to enter sympathetically into the experiences of other men and women. Third, the extent to which we think about these two.

Of the three, personal experience is the first essential. A being without personal experience would be less than a person. But experience, of itself, is no guarantee of wisdom. Most of us are ignorant in spite of experience. When we see a man repeating an earlier folly, we are quick to pass the judgment, "He'll never learn!" But what about us? Do we give other people cause to say the same thing about us? Do we ever say it of ourselves? Do we admit that we fail to profit by experience? If we do, are we honest enough to go one stage further, and say that the main reason for this is the fact that we are too lazy to reflect upon our experiences?

We all possess the ability to enter sympathetically into the experiences of others, although we do not all possess this ability to the same degree. Yet even those who are best able and most ready to "rejoice with them that do rejoice, and weep with them that weep" (Romans 12:15) may be living on a purely emotional level. They may gain nothing at all from their relationships because they are due solely to glandular activity. The feeling part of our nature is the uncritical part of it.

Wisdom and insight come, not from the number of things we do, or from the poignancy of the things we feel, but from the way in which we think about them.

This is nowhere better illustrated than by Christmas. From our earliest days it has been a precious and exciting season for us. It may well be that the happiest memories, not only of our childhood, but of our whole life, are associated with this blessed time of the year. These memories include other people and the relationships with them into which we were able to enter because of the special nature of Christmas-time. But it is quite possible that while we have these wonderful memories, we have not really learned very much from them. In other words, we have not analyzed them seriously.

If this is true of our Christmas *experiences,* it is at least as true of the Christmas *story*. If the happy celebrations we have known have not increased our understanding of the meaning of life, has the event behind those celebrations done anything for us?

In this chapter I want us to think about the lovely Christmas story which we know so well, and see if we can relate it not only to our own lives, but also to the lives of others, and to God's purpose for us and for them in this amazing and perplexing twentieth century.

* * * * *

We hear a great deal today about "status symbols." I possess numerous dictionaries and several encyclopedias, but none of them contains a definition of this term. I assume that the omission was made deliberately, on the grounds that no one needs it, because everyone knows what it means.

Of all the people who have ever lived, Jesus was the only one who had the power to choose the status symbols He desired before He came to earth. He was the only one who was able to decide into what kind of class and family He would be born. He was the only one who was able to name His own birthplace.

Jesus chose to be born in the manger of a primitive barn. He chose poor people for His earthly parents. He chose an enemy-occupied country for His native land.

When He grew up, He chose underprivileged men to be His friends. So far as we know, He never owned a piece of property. He told a scribe who wished to follow Him, "The foxes have holes, and the birds of the heaven have nests; but the Son of Man hath not where to lay his head" (Matthew 8:20; Luke 9:58). When the temple-tax was demanded of Jesus and His disciples, they did not have half a shekel (Exodus 30:13) between them. They had to go fishing (Matthew 17:27) to raise the meager sum of less than fifty cents.

Yet the judgment of mankind upon Jesus is that He lived the fullest, richest, and most worth-while life this world has ever seen. Emerson said of Him, "The greatest man in history was the poorest."

Somerset Maugham is a brilliant man. He is one of the most successful of modern novelists. He is a multi-millionaire. "I have enjoyed every luxury that man can desire," is his confession.[1] His autobiography makes fascinating reading. Yet this is his bleak conclusion: "I have been asked on occasion whether I would be willing to live my life over again. On the

[1] *Extracts from "A Writer's Notebook"* in *Mr. Maugham Himself*, p. 683.

whole it has been a pretty good one, perhaps better than that of most people, but I should see no point in repeating it."[2]

Most people think Somerset Maugham "has everything." He has a home in London, a villa on the French Riviera, a welcome in the centers of sophisticated society, the adulation of millions, every status symbol a man could desire, everything, *except an understanding of the purpose of life.*

A man named George Burns lived in nineteenth-century industrial Britain. He dotted the Atlantic with the first steamships. When he was ninety-four years old, he was knighted by Queen Victoria. At that time he wrote, "Men say that mine has been a most prosperous career. It is true, and I am thankful for it. But, looking back upon life, as I do now, this reflection gives me no satisfaction: there is nothing in that fact on which I can rest. But when I read, as I have been reading lately, the letters written by myself seventy years ago, and when I find that, even then, I had definitely decided to serve Christ, that knowledge indeed rejoices my heart in my old age."[3]

Neither Somerset Maugham nor George Burns derived any permanent satisfaction from what they *had*. They both realized the tinsel nature of status symbols. But George Burns could enjoy real happiness because he had an understanding of the nature of life. It was this that made him what he *was*.

The message of Christmas surely is that the important thing is not what we *have*, but what we *are*. "We brought nothing into this world, and it is certain we can carry nothing out," and we are here for only a limited time.

Translators are always keenly aware that a certain something is frequently lost in passing from one language to another. In the King James version of the Bible we read, "The Word was made flesh, and dwelt among us" (John 1:14). In the original,

[2] *The Summing Up* in *Mr. Maugham Himself,* p. 677.
[3] F. W. Boreham, *The Crystal Pointers,* p. 109.

the expression is more vivid, "The Word was made flesh, and *tented* among us." The idea is that of a temporary sojourn. The author of the Epistle to the Hebrews (13:14) applies this principle to all Christ's followers.

We are strangers and pilgrims on earth. We have no abiding city here. Our citizenship is in heaven (Philippians 3:20). This determines our attitude toward status symbols as such, and also to the thing of which they are symbols. Our life here and now is but a period of preparation for a nobler and fuller life. We are fools if we clutter up this life with junk. If there is a characteristic of a pilgrim, it is the fact that he travels light.

Wherefore let us set
A watch upon ourselves while yet we hold
The reins of will to guide our spirit's choice;
Lest unawares life's chiefest word be "Self",
All thoughts revolving round it; and self-love,
Staining the substance of its central cell,
Color its very being; and inwrought,
As thread in web, a rotten selfishness
Ruin the whole.

—Amy W. Carmichael

* * * * *

I do not wish to make the mistake of regarding the material and the spiritual sides of life as distinct and separate. They are both interrelated and interdependent. Whatever the spiritual may consist of, there is no access to it except through the material. The real world is never encountered as either spiritual or material. Life is a unity.

Unfortunately, there are still people who say the Gospel has nothing to do with what they disdainfully call "secular" life. They ask, "What can religion possibly have to do with politics, economics, industry, or education?" People who talk like that do not stop to think that they are saying exactly the same thing as the Communists. They do not stop to think! The poor folks behind the Iron Curtain are told, "You may continue to hold your religious services, read your Bibles, say your prayers, and recite your creeds, so long as you recognize the fact that religion and the churches have nothing to do with the way the country is run, and the conditions under which you live and work." This is a monstrous heresy.

Neither do I want to fall into that other error which says that the material side of life is of small consequence, and only those things which we unctuously call "spiritual" are really worth worrying about. Let no one tell you that the material blessings of life are unimportant. Men and women grow less like children of God when they lack the basic necessities of life.

My family and I lived for some time on the lovely island of St. Kitts, where sugar is king. There was a great deal of labor unrest. The cane-cutters received 70c per day for six months out of the year. The rest of the time they were unemployed. There was no social security insurance of any kind. The absentee landlords drew fabulous profits from their sugar estates.

I discussed the distressing economic situation with one of the wealthiest men on the island. He obviously resented my questions. Rather brusquely, he said, "You don't understand how bitter these people are." The only reply of which I could think was, "*You* would be bitter if you had spent your life under their conditions."

To tell such people that the material side of life is unimportant is a gross sin. It is those who have to do without so many things who best know their value. We neglect the material things of life to the peril of the Gospel.

This is the accusation Communism levels at the Christian Church. It regards religion psychologically as mere wishful thinking, intellectually as the product of fear and ignorance, and historically as serving the interests of exploiters, whether kings, priests, or capitalists. While it is not difficult to refute the first two charges, there is too much truth in the third for our comfort.

Although Communism claims to disbelieve in God, it acts as if it did have some belief, while modern Christians all too often claim that they believe in God, but act as if they did not. "I often think," wrote C. G. Lang, "of the words of an earnest agnostic. He said, 'If I could believe one-tenth part of what you Christians profess, I think there is nothing I could not venture and suffer; and yet, when I go to your churches, how dull and tame and heavy you Christians seem.' "

It would certainly be ironic if a job which the Communists could not do for themselves should be done for them by the very people who profess to be their worst enemies.

Paul was never content until he got to Rome. If he were alive today, his heart would be set on getting to Moscow.

The Communists fall into the error of making the material side of life the whole of life, thus avoiding the pitfall of dualism, but ending up in as dangerous and untenable a position.

If it is dangerous to neglect the material things of life, it is both unfair and uncharitable to dismiss the plight of the needy as being the result of their own irresponsibility. It is unfair and uncharitable because it is untrue.

To say that the "haves" and the "have-nots" can often be traced back to the "dids" and the "did-nots," evades the issue, unless we are scrupulously careful to distinguish between "often" and "always."

The laborers on the sugar plantations never had a chance. They owned no land. There was no land to be bought, even if they had had the money with which to buy it. There were no "job opportunities." I often lay awake at night wondering how they managed to stay alive.

There is an understandable joy in possessions. Happiness based on *things* can be very real. If you watch a child's face on Christmas morning, you learn that. If you give your wife a washing-machine, she will surely rejoice that it takes some of the drudgery out of her life. If she says, "You shouldn't have!" she probably means, "You shouldn't have waited so long!"

The late Aga Kahn III, leader of the Ismaili Moslem sect, was fond of the pleasures of the table. When a visitor asked him how he reconciled his partiality for worldly enjoyments with his position as a religious leader, the Aga replied, "I do not think the Lord meant the good things of this world to be enjoyed only by sinners."

There are many choice Christians of our day who find that sensitivity to beauty is a soul-window open towards God; that earth's fair things can and do minister to very deep needs and longings. With Keats they know that,

In spite of all
Some shape of beauty moves away the pall
From our dark spirits. Such the sun, the moon,
Trees old and young, sprouting a shady boon
For simple sheep; and such are daffodils
With the green world they live in; and clear rills
That for themselves a cooling covert make
'Gainst the hot season;
All lovely tales that we have heard or read,
An endless fountain of immortal drink,
Pouring into us from the heaven's brink.

This must not lead us to the unfortunate situation in which we need these props to such an extent that we bestow upon them an exaggerated emphasis. When *things* loom too large on life's horizon, they defeat the very purpose for which they were intended. Instead of being our servants, they become our masters.

Once upon a time, there was a man who loved money for money's sake. Over the years he accumulated a huge fortune, which delighted his miserly heart. He would walk a mile in the rain to save a nickel. One day his wife returned from visiting her physician and said rather timidly, as the wives of skinflints are wont to do, "I was at the doctor's today, and he ordered a change in climate." "That's fine," replied her niggardly husband, "according to the weather-report, it's coming tomorrow."

Although the material things of life may bring joy, it is a grievous mistake to identify happiness with possessions. It is not what we *have* that makes us happy. It is what we *are*.

The United States, Great Britain, and France have the highest standards of living in the world. They have the finest educational systems. Their technological abilities are phenomenal. Their physical health is well cared for. Every year the people can expect to live longer. Personal incomes have risen to an all-time high. Yet these three nations lead the world in alcoholism, suicides, divorces, juvenile delinquency, and mental illness. They have forgotten that guided mortals are more important than guided missiles.

It is a strange fact of modern life that the psychiatrists' offices are filled with people who belong to that section of the community which is regarded as the most prosperous. They have everything — *except a reason for living.*

You can get a great deal of happiness from the material things of life, so long as you do not identify happiness with success. You can have all the status symbols an acquisitive society can invent, and yet know in your own heart that your life is empty of meaning. It is not what we *have,* but what we *are,* that really counts.

We cannot know our world until we find
A compass that can chart the world we know.

What do we know? We are a kindly people,
And when we see a wrong we try to right it.
A boy run over in the street by a car
Finds mothers, grandmothers, at once to help him;
He's laid on cushions till the doctor comes,
And family lace is used to wipe his cuts.
We are very tender, most kind, about physical pain.

At all times we are very kind to dogs;
If our canaries die, we are unconsoled.
We go to church, we fumble in our pockets
For coins to give to newsboys and to God;
We make good coffee; we go to cheerful movies;
At weddings our eyes are filled with simple tears.
We like waffles and syrup; we praise gas,
We praise coal, we praise inventiveness;
We admire the mysterious men who work all day
Holding test-tubes up against the light,
Who will revolutionize the rubber industry;
When we come home at night we kiss our wives
But we do not see their faces; when we wake
In the smart morning we are fresh for a new day,
Because we know that in the bathroom cupboard
Are toothpaste, mouthwash, razor-blades and kleenex.

Is this our world? Or only half our world?
Loving our world, what shall we do to keep it?
Loving our world, what shall we do to find
Its deeper heart, which only keeps us whole?[4]

[4] *Challenge,* Copyright 1943 by The New Yorker Magazine, Inc., may be used only by permission.

* * * * *

There can be no doubt that there are certain things in life we all seek. Food, clothing, and shelter are among their number. Jesus never condemned the search for these things. He said quite plainly, "Your heavenly Father knoweth that ye have need of all these things" (Matthew 6:32; Luke 12:30). What He did condemn was the anxiety which pushes these things to the forefront of our thinking and acting. "Put God first" was the basic condition Jesus laid down for getting all we need in *this* life.

Modern thinking is a complete reversal of this. People today imagine that being a Christian is a matter of subtraction. They think they must give up this thing, forego that thing, avoid the other thing.

Jesus says that it is a process of addition, "Seek ye first the kingdom of God and his righteousness; and all these things *shall be added unto you*" (Matthew 6:33).

Although we may not be aware of it, the majority of us are people of faith. Each day we live on the assurance of God's dependability. Even those who make no claim to faith order their lives on the assumption that there is law and order in the universe, that is, on the assumption that God is dependable.

Isn't this the message of Christmas? The birth of Jesus tells us that God keeps His promises. This is God's world, and He orders it.

Jesus says, "Put God first," not only because that is where He belongs, but also because that is the purpose of life. The real significance of life is to be a means of communication between God and man. It is to be a revelation of God. Behind and above our changing sense-experience and the meaning it has for our immediate activity, there is "the land of far distances." There is "the King in His beauty."

Christmas tells us that life is meant to be fellowship with

God, that in that fellowship is our highest good and truest happiness, and that Jesus was born in Bethlehem of Judea in the days of Herod the king to make that fellowship possible.

As we observe another anniversary of our Lord's birth, it should jolt us to an awareness of our true condition and create within us a deep sense of dissatisfaction.

Dissatisfaction is both a medicine of the soul and a tonic to the mind. If peace, quiet, and satisfaction with the *status quo* had been the ideal of all men, we would still be slaves. We would still be tied to the land. We would still believe in a flat earth. Witches and heretics would still be burnt at the stake, as a fearsome warning to others who "had ideas." Magic and home-made remedies of toads' entrails would still "cure" small-pox or warts. We would still be traveling at the speed of a horse upon the land, and of the wind upon the sea. The air would be only for us to breathe. People who talked about flying would be sent to Bedlam.

Dissatisfaction is the seed of progress. But it must be dissatisfaction through illumination. No one has expressed it more beautifully than Browning:

Just when we are safest, there's a sunset touch,
A fancy from a flower-bell, someone's death,
A chorus ending from Euripides,
And that's enough for fifty hopes and fears
As old and new at once as nature's self.

This is dissatisfaction, not with what we *have,* but with what we *are.*

10

"Emmanuel...God With Us"

—Matthew 1:23

CHRISTMAS ASSURES US THAT GOD IS IN THIS LIFE. HE IS not only *behind* it and *above* it. He is *in* it. His redemptive purpose does not *underlie* it. It *permeates* it.

Because God is *in* this life, we have life, "and have it more abundantly" (John 10:10). But this abundant life is not for our own satisfaction. We are "saved to serve." The brand plucked from the burning is to become the light to lighten the Gentiles.

Christmas is not man seeking God. Christmas is God seeking man. It is not God seeking man for a life of passive fellowship. It is God seeking man for a life of active co-operation. The perfect wisdom of love seeks a partnership.

Jesus was born in Bethlehem of Judea, not to remove life's burdens, but to strengthen us to bear them; not to do away with life's crosses, but to enable us to carry them; not to eliminate life's battles, but to give us victory in them.

At Christmas time we concentrate so much on "peace on

earth among men with whom he is well pleased" (Luke 2:14) that we lose sight of that other provoking declaration, "I came not to send peace, but a sword" (Matthew 10:34).

We are facing in the wrong direction if we see only the Babe of Bethlehem. Indeed, we are facing in the wrong direction if we see only the Man of Galilee. It is not enough for us to reverence the Jesus of history. We must have an experience of the Christ of today. Ours is a Saviour who was not only born, dead, and buried, but is "alive for evermore" (Revelation 1:18).

Our Christmas adoration is spurious if it ends at the Manger. It has to go on to a Lord who is *always* seeking for our homage, our devotion and our service. God's demand is not only up to the minute, it is also out to the limit. It is impossible to be a saint on your knees if you are a sinner on your feet. Indeed, you cannot honestly pray about any situation unless you are prepared to do something about it yourself. You cannot atone to God for breaking His laws by erecting churches in His honor.

Dr. George MacCleod tells the story of a boy who threw a stone through a stained-glass window which portrayed the birth of the Christ-Child. In capital letters it bore the inscription:

GLORY TO GOD IN THE HIGHEST.

The boy's stone knocked out the second letter *E.* So until the window was repaired, it read:

GLORY TO GOD IN THE HIGH ST.,

which is the real message of Christmas.

The peril of celebrating Christmas in the traditional manner is that we may imagine it has nothing to do with the daily round and common task. It has everything to do with it. It is the assurance that human experience need frighten us no more. It is the promise of God Himself that no sacrifice or suffering need be in vain. It is God coming to be with us to show us that He *cares.* It is the source of Dora Greenwell's penetrating motto, *Et teneo et teneor* — "I both hold and am held."

Many people believe in "The Great Perhaps." Some folks say that to whatever gods there be we are like the flies that boys kill on a summer's day.

No! such a god my worship may not win,
Who lets the world about his fingers spin,
A thing extern: My God must rule within,
And whom I own for Father, God, Creator,
Hold Nature in Himself, Himself in Nature;
And in His kindly arms embraced, the whole
Doth live and move by His pervading soul.

—Goethe

Christmas assures us that the lowly sparrows do not lose a feather that has not been brushed away by the finger of God. It tells us that we are never alone. God walks beside us in every struggle. He is with us even when we know it not.

He hides Himself so wondrously
As though there were no God,
He is least seen when all the powers
Of ill are most abroad.
Thrice blest is he to whom is given
The instinct that can tell
That God is on the field when He
Is most invisible.

—F. W. Faber

* * * * *

Christmas speaks to us of Christ's coming. But, as has been pointed out so often, He came *to remain.* It is this that makes every day "Christmas Day." It is this that makes every day "Christ's Day." It is this that makes every day a "Day of Hope."

Hope, like the gleaming taper's light,
Adorns and cheers our way;
And still, as darker grows the night,
Emits a brighter ray.
—Oliver Goldsmith

Christian Hope rests upon what we know of God through Jesus Christ. It springs out of faith in Him as Lord of all. It is the result of confidence in His utter trustworthiness.

Sir Christopher Wren fell out with the city fathers of Windsor. He had been retained to build a great corn market. He presented a design which showed no pillars supporting the roof. The aldermen could not conceive of such a thing. They insisted on pillars. Finally, the enraged architect yielded to their demands. He agreed to give them pillars, although he still argued that they were unnecessary. Many years later, it was found he had won after all. He had made the pillars one half-inch shorter than the roof. There they stand, but they serve no useful purpose, for the roof has never sagged.

Hope is simply the recognition that the Great Architect of the universe knows what He is doing. It is the certainty that evil will eventually be destroyed. It is the perception that Goodness, Beauty and Truth are eternal. They must finally prevail over all that hinders or opposes us in our search for the Good Life, because they are of the nature of Almighty God Himself.

There never shall be lost one good! What was shall live as before;
The evil is null, is naught, is silence implying sound;
What was good, shall be good, with, for evil, so much good more;

On the earth the broken arcs; in the heaven a perfect round.
All we have willed or hoped or dreamed of good, shall exist;
Not its semblance, but itself; no beauty, nor good, nor power
Whose voice has gone forth, but each survives for the melodist
Whose eternity affirms the conception of an hour.
The high that proved too high, the heroic for earth too hard,
The passion that left the ground to lose itself in the sky,
Are music sent up to God by the lover and the bard;
Enough that He heard it once; we shall hear it by-and-by.
And what is our failure here but a triumph's evidence
For the fulness of the days? Have we withered and agonized?
Why else was the pause prolonged, but that singing might issue thence?
Why rushed the dischords in, but that Harmony should be prized?

—Robert Browning

If, this Christmas, we see His Star, then by its light we can walk all our days in righteousness and peace. If, this Christmas, our hearts sing, "Glory to God in the Highest," then our lives will proclaim, "Glory to God in the High St." If, this Christmas, we make the journey to Bethlehem as pilgrims, then we can go our way into an unknown future with the quietness, confidence, and "patience of hope."

We need hope. It broadens our outlook. It pours the wine of joy into our hearts, evokes new powers within our souls, liberates our energies, develops our thought, fires our zeal, strengthens our wills, fortifies our convictions, renews our determination. And — make no mistake about it — *determination* is what we need just now.

* * * * *

The ancient Greeks were profound students of human nature. They showed this in the word which they used for *man*. "Man," they said, "is *anthropos,*" and that word means, quite simply, "the animal with the upward look." We become ourselves, so the Greeks taught, when we look up.

Biologically, we may be akin to the rest of the animal creation. Psychologically and spiritually, there is something distinctive about us. We have the capacity for looking up. Unfortunately, as we have seen, we do not always employ it, for it takes effort. It is too much for some of us.

If you want an easy life, don't be different from your neighbors. The commonplace and the stupid have the easiest life of all. That, I suppose, is the basic reason for the vogue of conformity. It takes no effort at all. But, as Henry Van Dyke pointed out, "Individuality is the salt of common life. You may have to live in a crowd, but you do not have to live like it, nor subsist on its food."[1]

If we are what we ought to be, we are creatures of aspiration. Man, when he is truly himself, is a restless being. He is always seeking new heights. Time after time he reaches a height he had mistaken for the summit. There is always a peak beyond it, towering above it. He finds there is always a height beyond the height, so he keeps on.

He is perpetually agitating after something better and nobler than he already knows. The Promised Land always lies on the other side of a wilderness, but the wilderness does not daunt him.

He may, however, be dismayed when he reads these lines from a modern industrialist, who says that if man is to succeed, "First, he has to have his eye on the ball, his back to the wall, and his ear to the ground. Then he is expected to put his shoulder to the wheel, his nose to the grindstone, keep a level head and both feet on the ground, at the same time look for the silver lining!"

We show ourselves to be men when we have the upward look. When we lose the upward look, we forfeit our highest

[1] *The School of Life,* p. 33.

name. It is not easy to maintain the upward look day after day, month after month. The successful life is always the life of discipline.

The heights by great men reached and kept
Were not attained by sudden flight,
But they, while their companions slept,
Were toiling upward in the night.

—Longfellow

Holman Hunt worked for three years on "The Light of the World." He always worked out of doors, and at night. He painted by the light of a candle. To keep his feet warm, he wrapped them in straw. No price was too great if only he could create "The Light of the World."

Have you ever heard of Henry Wallin? He lived in Cambridge. He was so badly crippled that when he went to Harvard it took him seven years to complete his course. He had to be wheeled from class to class in a chair. He was in constant physical pain. But in spite of that pain he made himself expert in deciphering ancient Pali manuscripts. His pain was so great that he could not sit to write. He had to work standing before a high desk, with his crutches under his arms. When he could endure the agony no longer, he knelt in front of a chair in order to take the strain off his back. Out of such circumstances came his famous translation of the Buddhist scriptures. One of the world's highest Buddhists paid a visit to Cambridge to bring Henry Wallin the thanks of India.

In the midst of his disability and anguish, because of his *determination,* Henry Wallin found happiness, success and fame.

Of wounds and sore defeat
I made my battle stay;
Winged sandals for my feet
I wove of my delay;

Of weariness and fear
I made my shouting spear,
Of loss and doubt and dread
And swift oncoming doom
I made a helmet for my head
And a flowing plume.
From the shutting mist of death,
From the failure of the breath
I made a battle horn to blow
Across the vales of overthrow.
O hearken, love, the battle horn!
The triumph clear, the silver scorn:
O hearken where the Echoes bring
Down the gray disastrous morn
Laughter and rallying.

—William V. Moody

Robert Louis Stevenson might have written that. In the whole of his life he never enjoyed a full week free from the threat of the sick-bed. It was in a period of acute suffering that he penned the joyous lines:

The world is so full of a number of things,
I'm sure we should all be as happy as kings.

Theodore Roosevelt was a great man. Underlying his greatness was the positive Christian philosophy which he expressed in the now famous words, "I wish to preach not the doctrine of ignoble ease, but the doctrine of the strenuous life."

Without sustained effort we stagnate. The religion worth having is that which acts as a spur to energy, and directs that energy most productively. This is the religion of Christmas — "God with us." It is the consequence of realizing that God is *in* this world, and *in us*.

To know
Rather consists in opening out a way
Whence the imprisoned splendor may escape,
Than in effecting entry for a light
Supposed to be without.
—Robert Browning

Because we do not understand this, we often face a great purpose in a wrong mood. Our courage withers under the pressure of self-pity. We forget whose world this is. We forget whose we are and whom we serve. The challenge is always there — but so is Almighty God.

Do not shirk difficulties. Do not evade responsibilities or seek to escape burden-bearing. There is no victory in withdrawal. Do not covet the job which demands the least of you. This is a monstrous attitude. To adopt it as a policy means ruin. It starves the intellect, poisons the conscience, enervates the will, destroys manhood. It guarantees failure because it forgets "God with us."

Few men in the history of the Christian Church have had deeper insight into things that matter than Bishop Phillips Brooks. Perhaps you recall his challenging words, "Do not pray for easy lives; pray to be stronger men. Do not pray for tasks equal to your powers; pray for powers equal to your tasks."

Not for us are content, and quiet, and peace of mind,
For we go seeking a city that we shall never find.
Only the road, and the dawn, the sun, and the wind, and the rain,
And the watchfire under the stars, and sleep, and the road again.
We travel the dusty road, till the light of the day is dim,
And the sunset shows us spires, away on the world's rim.
—John Masefield

We need more than guts for this. We need an understanding of "Emmanuel, God with us." During the Advent season, let us pray:

O holy God, I ask this boon of Thee: —
Be mine, in truth, a soul that worships; free
From all profane and trivial thoughts, and filled
With reverential faith; a soul all stilled
In hush of awe; since Thou, the God most high,
To lowly, contrite men, art ever nigh.

—Carey Bonner

11

Joy to the World

WHEN THE HERALD ANGEL SAID, "BEHOLD, I BRING YOU good tidings of great joy" (Luke 2:10), he uttered the message for which the world was waiting.

"Good tidings of great joy." That's what we want. That's why Christmas is such a popular season. The spirit of Christmas is the spirit of Joy.

This applies in a very special way to children. We are not far wrong when we say that Christmas is their festival. It has to be, because He whose holy birth we remember at this blessed time came into the world as one of them. This is their season, their time to be merry. Perhaps that is why one little boy, when asked what he would like for Christmas, replied, "I would like something that will separate the men from the toys!"

Christmas is the most human and lovable of all the Church feasts. Easter celebrates a victory in which we had no part. The majestic glory of the Risen Christ sets Him apart from us. Pentecost commemorates the mysterious coming of the Holy Spirit, an event so shrouded in misunderstanding that this major festival has been relegated to minor status in many churches. When, on All Saints' Day, we are somehow reminded of the cold purity of the Hellenic marbles, we become grateful for All Souls' Day! But even that gets away from us. We can never escape Christmas just because it is so homey.

The Baby, the Manger, the Shepherds, and the Star are not subjects which interest only specialists and experts. They appeal to the best natural affections of all of us.

No one feels it is out of place to speak of "A Merry Christmas." It is a greeting which is on all our lips at this season. It receives an emphasis which shows it is heartfelt. It is a phrase which conjures up a multitude of precious memories. We think of carol-singers and of candle-light services where people who do not regard themselves as particularly "religious" greet the birth of the Divine Child in time-honored strains, and enjoy themselves thoroughly as they do so.

We think of family gatherings, of feastings and revelries, of gifts we have received and presents we have given, of horse-play and practical jokes in which we have indulged, and of some very wonderful lessons we have learned. It is indeed a curious medley. The merriment and the good cheer, the decorated tree and the lighted candle, the tinkling bells and the resounding music, these are the expressions of a spirit which, while not forgetting the Divine side of our Lord's birthday, yet delights in its simple humanity. This spirit enabled my friend Mr. W. T. Keener to write to me one Christmas:

To Wish You

"AN OLD-FASHIONED CHRISTMAS"

"Backward, turn backward, O Time in thy flight"
To an old-fashioned Christmas, just for tonight.
Sleighbells aringing, folks at the door,
Minstrels asinging for pennies or more.
Candlelights gleaming out through the snow,

Children just beaming at stockings hung low.
Holly and Mistletoe, tinsel that shines,
Winds that whistle low through the pines.
Church bells intoning carols so sweet,
Tables just groaning with good things to eat:
Pumpkin and mincemeat, all kinds of pie,
Cakes that you eat with a gleam in your eye,
Baked ham and turkey, gravy and rice,
Dressing that whispered of oysters and spice,
Fluffy potatoes, succulent corn,
Biscuits as light as a breeze in the morn,
Baked yams and chestnuts. Oh! What a sight!
Sillabub, foaming and frosty and white.
And over it all, so loving and warm
Stood Mother, the symbol of welcome and charm.

Dear Lord, that's a picture so hallowed and dear,
A memory that quickens with Time in her flight.
We'd give all our modern, commercialized cheer
Just for an old-fashioned Christmas to-night.

The spirit that links the birth of Jesus to the common life of the common people, that brings human happiness into religion — this, in truth, is "the spirit of Christmas."

* * * * *

The desire for happiness is born in us. It is part and parcel of our human make-up. It is so fundamental to our nature that no power can destroy it. When Hitler was ruler of Germany, he forbade his people to celebrate Christmas. In spite of his supreme authority and the perverted veneration in which the gullible populace held him, his order was widely disobeyed. No tyrant can take from us the desire to be happy. It is something God has planted in our hearts.

The Constitution of these United States guarantees to everyone certain "inalienable rights," among which is spelled out "the pursuit of happiness." Neither the Bible nor the Christian Church has any quarrel either with that statement or with the high humanitarian ideal which it embodies.

As Christians, we do not despise happiness. Nor do we scorn pleasure. A great deal of harm has been done to the cause of Jesus by that narrow super-puritanical zeal which wears a long face. We remember that our Master prayed for His disciples "that they might have my joy fulfilled in themselves" (John 17:13).

The Church was born into a world in which the dominant emotion was fear. Dr. T. R. Glover says that one of the important reasons for the rapid growth of Christianity was the joy which was characteristic of the early disciples.

The Church is the herald of glad tidings. It is the comforter of those who mourn. It is the healer of the broken-hearted. It is the mediator of cheerfulness and courage.

The joy of the Lord contains the true interpretation of life. It offers the light we need for our feet, the strength for our moral struggles, and the solace for our troubles. Christians cannot be "kill-joys," for they are commanded to "Rejoice in the Lord" (Philippians 3:1; 4:4; etc.).

So, in spite of the chaotic conditions of the world, in spite of bitterness and hatred, in spite of misunderstandings and confusion, men and women long for peace and goodwill. Their pulses quicken when they hear again the angelic proclamation, "I bring you good tidings of great joy."

Unfortunately, the search for happiness is often pursued along wrong lines. Indeed, *seeking* happiness does not produce it. This is one of the apparent contradictions of life. If you want to be wealthy, you must pursue riches. You must apply yourself to that one end. You must allow nothing to interfere with your ambition. If you want to be learned, you have no choice but to dedicate yourself to a hard and continuous study which permits very little time for anything else. You must *give yourself* to your task. But it is not so with happiness. Pursue it, and it evades you at every turn. Seek it resolutely, and it becomes a veritable jack-o'-lantern. If, above everything in this world, you crave happiness, and if you direct your every energy to that goal, it is the one thing you will never know.

And yet, if Christmas says anything to us, it is, surely, that our heavenly Father wants all His earthly children to find their desire for happiness fulfilled.

But does Christmas say anything to us? When we were children it spoke to us with a very clear voice. Has our familiarity with the Advent theme dulled, or even deadened, our sense of hearing?

If Christmas no longer speaks to us, is it because we have come to take it for granted? If we have, that means we have come to take the birth of Jesus for granted, like the rising of the sun or the coming of spring.

We take it for granted that the sun rises every morning. There are learned scientists and astronomers who can explain, with mathematical exactness, why the sunrise must occur. It is part of the natural order of things. In the kind of universe we inhabit, it could not be otherwise.

But you cannot put the birth of Jesus into this category. This is something that need not have happened. Whatever else it is, "It is the gift of God." "For ye know the *grace* of our Lord Jesus Christ, that though he was rich, yet for your sakes he became poor" (2 Corinthians 8:9). There could be no possible compulsion that He who dwells "in light inaccessible, hid from our eyes," should gate-crash into history.

Nothing could force Him to make Himself "of no reputation," and to be "found in fashion as a man." Nothing could coerce Him to be born in the squalor of a stable. *Constraint* does not enter into this, only *Love*.

It was Love that led "the Creator of the ends of the earth"

to express Himself in terms of time and sense. It was Love that led Almighty God to utter Himself in the language of humanity, "the Word made flesh."

Love came down at Christmas,
Love all lovely, Love divine.

It was Love which determined the form He would take, the rank He would assume, and the way He would work while He was here on earth.

As He lay a new-born and helpless Baby in His Virgin Mother's arms, the number of people who saw anything extraordinary about Him was, so far as we know, extremely small. The madding crowds in Bethlehem were certainly not diverted from whatever they were doing to celebrate their family reunions by the pathetic birth in a cave on the outskirts of the town.

When He first appeared by the waters of Gennesaret, He was apparently just another man. No unusual claims were made for Him, and He made none for Himself.

But when they watched Him and marked His words, and perceived the Spirit that was in Him, they realized that He saw what they did not see, that He could do what they could not do. The day came when He touched the cord-strings of the heart as no one had ever touched them, and they said there was something in Him that made Him different.

His own Beatitudes catch a fleeting glimpse of that something. But He Himself was greater than His Beatitudes. He was the ideal made real. He was the personification of ideal goodness, ideal mercy, ideal wisdom, and ideal love. When Paul wrote 1 Corinthians 13, he was thinking of Jesus.

Yet He was clothed in such humble, human garb that a woman with an unsavory past could talk with Him quite naturally at the side of a well (John 4:7ff.), and a shy and patient sufferer could wriggle through an unsympathetic crowd to touch the hem of His garment (Mark 5:30; Luke 8:43f.).

This "Joy of man's desiring" did not go about wearing a halo. Still less did He strike a pose before an audience. His love of feasts was so proverbial that gossip said He was "a gluttonous man and a winebibber" (Matthew 11:19; Luke 7:34). It must have been extremely difficult to recognize the Son of God in a Galilean peasant.

His scorn was reserved for those who made a parade of religion. The people He denounced were those who counted themselves among "the choice spirits," those who prided themselves on being "the best people," and those who delighted to receive the homage of those who could not afford to offend City Hall. Outwardly, He was a simple Man, and the simple people loved Him.

* * * * *

Unfortunately, when men began their attempts to explain Jesus, when they began to analyze Him and to say of what His personality was composed, they got completely off the track. They divided Him up. They said one part of Him was human and another part was Divine. Instead of the beautiful and clear Figure of the Gospels, they created a strange and mysterious being who did not belong to this earthly scene at all. The outline of His face became shadowy. The tone of His voice seemed remote and alien. He was enshrouded in a magical veil which mortal eyes could not pierce. We may say without hesitation that the Latin Church developed such a grotesque caricature of the Jesus of History that He has no contact at all with human life and need, and so they elevated His Blessed Mother to fill the gap which they had created.

It was this false image of Jesus which caused Francis Palgrave to cry:

Comes faint and far Thy voice
From vales of Galilee;
The vision fades in ancient shades;
How should we follow Thee?

But if we turn from the Schoolmen to the artists, the tale is different. This is particularly true of Christmas. Our healthiest impressions of the Advent have been formed by pictures.

The Shepherds on the one side, the three Kings from the East on the other, united in adoration of the newly-born Child in the midst, are cónstant elements of a variously represented scene, familiar to us through the skill and devotion of several generations of painters.

We rightly talk of "the simplicity of Christmas," but we must not forget that it has its complex side too.

If there were signs of poverty and lowliness round the makeshift cradle, there were signs of splendor and majesty as well. If His parents were poor, they were of royal blood. If He was "the seed of the woman," He was also "the Son of God." If His birthplace was "little among the thousands of Judah," it was great in historic memories and ancient predictions. If His cradle was a manger, it was an altar before which Wise Men worshipped. If He was born in a stable, it was irradiated by the Star of a King.

The angel said, "Behold, I bring you good tidings of great joy." This is not the message of Christmas. It is the prologue to it. Without the "good tidings" there is no "joy." The good tidings are, "Unto you is born this day in the city of David, a Saviour, which is Christ the Lord" (Luke 2:11).

Joy to the world!
The Lord is come.

The greatest thing that ever happened in this world happened in Bethlehem. Jesus was born.

"Christianity is simply Christ. It is this Person, presented to the intelligence and conscience of mankind, for each to accept and believe in. The Person, however, is not sufficiently described when His characteristics are delineated. His offer of Himself to men is part of His Person. His redemptive power for and over men is also part of His Person. The image of God reflected in His consciousness is part of His Person. The promise and power of spiritual continuance after His death, and of active operation in human life to "the end of the world," are part of His Person. Thus we obtain as the essence of Christianity the fact of Christ, a Person who is, in the first place, the ideal character, presented to mankind for following and imitation; in the second place, a living and eternal power accessible in the Spirit to the spirit of every man, a power to change and save every soul that receives Him; and in the third place, a mirror in which the Infinite and Eternal Being that made the world and man is sufficiently reflected."[1]

Is there any wonder that the Chinese word for "Gospel" is made up of two words which literally mean "Happiness from on High"?

Because God wants His people to be happy, He sent His only begotten Son to remove the cause of their unhappiness. The Beloved Disciple is very emphatic about this: "He was manifested to take away our sins" (1 John 3:5). "For this purpose the Son of God was manifested, that he might destroy the works of the devil" (1 John 3:8). This is the Christmas proclamation. These are "the good tidings of great joy." This is the only way to happiness and peace. This is the secret of "the joy of the Lord."

Such joy is more than that lightheartedness which withers at the first touch of trouble. It remains undimmed through long experience of pain. Men and women who have had heavy burdens to bear come to the end with hearts serene and glad as any child's. This securer brightness is a gift of our Lord to His friends. He so greatly loved children that He wished His followers to grow old without losing the child's heart.

If we will accept this gift we shall find that, in Christ, God

[1] Robert F. Horton, *Great Issues,* pp. 60f.

has prepared for us things more wonderful than the eye or ear of history has ever seen or heard; or that the heart of the most optimistic philosophy has ever dared to feel.

Three hundred years before Jesus was born, Archimedes, a Greek mathematician, physicist, and inventor, made a statement which has been quoted many times, "Give me a lever long enough, and a fulcrum strong enough, and single-handed I will move the world." It is the typical word of a man who sees the world only in terms of a physical mass. It has been a popular idea with those who have worshipped force. But Joseph Conrad was right when he said, "Don't talk to me of your Archimedes lever . . . but give me the right word and the right accent and I will move the world."

It is not the right argument, nor the right formula, nor the right equation that we need now. It is the right word and the right accent. There is such a Word. When it became flesh and dwelt on earth, it was seen to be Grace and Truth. It has become the lost Word of our nuclear Space Age. Therein lies tragedy and the joylessness of our times. The Word is unchanged. It can still meet man's every need. It is still the Word of Power, of Peace, of Joy in believing. It is up to us to find the accent which will convince men of its authority and its relevance. We can make this discovery at Christmas.

O come to us, abide with us, Our Lord Emmanuel.

EPILOGUE

Keeping the Spirit of Christmas

THERE IS A RAPTURE ABOUT CHRISTMAS WHICH KINDLES and delights all our hearts. It is a happy festival, for grown-ups as well as for children.

For a brief time we seem to pass out of our dull routine into an exciting world of song and drama, of Shepherds and Wise Men. In their fascinating company, we come to the Manger. With them, we bow before the Babe who was God's Love-Gift to the whole world. We sing our carols joyfully, and feel better for it. They help to draw our minds away from the humdrum affairs of our ordinary lives.

But when it is over, we have to go back to the commonplace things. We have to wrestle again with those same tasks and problems from which we were able to relax for a few festive days.

When the scenes from the Nativity Play are ended, the curtains have to come down. The Wise Men and the Shepherds have to take off their beards. They must change back into their regular clothes. They may do so with a sigh of relief, yet surely not without a pang of regret also.

Isn't that how we feel sometimes about the Christmas season itself? Don't we fear it is only temporary? Aren't we half persuaded that it is too artificial to last?

It is only a break. It is welcome enough, of course, but its influence is fleeting. We cannot remain at the Manger, any more than the Shepherds, the Wise Men, and the Holy Family could. The Shepherds had to go back to their sheep. The Wise Men had to return to their exotic East. Joseph had to take Jesus and Mary to Egypt for safety.

We, too, have to leave the Manger. We have to deal with the much less romantic and far more prosaic situation of preparing for a New Year, with all its uncertainties, misgivings, and fears.

However, are we committed to the view that Christmas is over because the celebrations have come to an end? Is it without significance that New Year follows so closely upon Christmas? Is there not something we can carry over from the festive season that will help to meet our need as we confront a new year? If Christmas is really over, then we ought to ask ourselves if it is worth all the time and effort we put into it.

If, through all the gay jubilations, we have heard the Nativity message and caught the Advent spirit, then Christmas is by no means over. Indeed, it may well be just beginning. We can still follow the Star, as it leads us *from* the Manger, back to our familiar, drab, ordinary surroundings.

If we have caught the spirit of Christmas, then life can never be the same again. The Child in the Manger is the reason. He is God's answer to all our misgivings. He is the guarantee that Light is greater than darkness. He is the proof that Courage is nobler than fear. He is the pledge that Hope is stronger than despair. He is the assurance that "Love never faileth."

The coming of Jesus was not intended to enliven us for a

few days each year. He was not born to provide a temporary escape from the monotonous affairs of human life. He came to bring a new spirit into the world.

So we are at our best at Christmas time. The spirit of reconciliation is abroad. Feelings of ill-will are thrust aside. There is less self-seeking. We would rather give than receive. Cynicism about human nature evaporates as people appear better than we thought. It is the happiest time we know.

The rest of the year we live "on our guard." We are afraid to lower our defenses. We have to keep up with the Joneses. At any rate, we have to make them think we are keeping up with them. There can be no let-up there.

During the rest of the year we can behave quite decently so long as our personal interests are not threatened. We can maintain our poise if we are not crossed. We can be amiable so long as we get our own way. We can show the Christmas spirit if we do not lose anything by it.

Unfortunately, it is easy to argue that this is due to "the kind of world in which we live." Our mid-twentieth century seems to be sympathetic only to those who are self-centered and on their guard. It respects only those who look after themselves. If you want to get anywhere, if you want to be anybody, you must keep this in mind constantly. The important question is always, "How is this going to affect *me*?"

There is a very definite answer to this kind of argument. It is an answer which begins with the recognition that this world isn't all it's cracked up to be. It is an answer which says this is a miserable world because selfishness, greed, and materialism have usurped the place which rightly belongs to the Christmas spirit.

How many people today enjoy real satisfaction? How many know the feeling of enduring security? Why are psychiatrists' waiting-rooms full of people *whose material possessions are the envy of their neighbors?*

Yet, at Christmas, when we enjoy giving more than receiving, we experience a singular sense of happiness, peace and satisfaction. *At Christmas, life is what it is intended to be three hundred sixty-five days a year.*

If we are as reasonable as we say we are, why do we dispense so readily with the Christmas spirit when we turn from the festive season to the business of everyday life?

* * * * *

It is the Christian belief that much of what is wrong with the world today is moral and spiritual. In other words, the spirit of Christmas is absent.

Perhaps those of us who profess and call ourselves Christians are to blame to some extent. We have allowed a Church Festival to become a pagan celebration. The Christmas spirit is missing from a great deal of *our* Christmas activity. The poor, exhausted, weary world surveys the mad rush of Christmas Eve, and wonders what it is all about, and if it can possibly be worth it.

We need to recover the theology of the Incarnation. Our people need to be steeped in it. They need to know what Christmas is all about — from God's point of view. If we are ever to get to the place where we can keep the spirit of Christmas, a lot depends upon our preachers.

Of course "Christmas is the festival of the home." We thank God that it is. Unfortunately, many homes are not too inspiring, even at Christmas. The decorations are there, and the tree, the Christmas angel, the turkey, and the presents. But because there is no theology there, the spirit of prayer and praise, of wonder and worship, of true *Christian* thanksgiving, is strangely lacking.

The children thank their parents and relatives. The parents and relatives thank their neighbors and friends. There is gratitude in their hearts as they show their presents one to another and boast about them on their way to the ball game. But how many give thanks to Almighty God for His Unspeakable Gift?

* * * * *

The Christmas story has captured the imagination of all sorts of people in all walks of life. I believe it has done more than this. I believe that for a few fleeting minutes we have managed to catch its spirit.

Perhaps as we have listened to the inspired music of the "Messiah"; perhaps as we have sung the familiar words of a best-loved carol; perhaps as once again we have heard the majestic prose-poetry of Luke's incomparable Nativity Story; perhaps as, like Mary, we have pondered these things in our hearts; perhaps as we have recounted them to our children — there has flashed upon the inward eye an unforgettable vision of "the exceeding great glory," so that, in the true spirit of Christmas, we have sung with Martin Luther:

My heart for very joy doth leap,
My lips no more can silence keep:
I, too, must sing with joyful tongue
That sweetest ancient cradle song.

And then we have awakened. Then we have come down to earth. We have gone out into the world, and failed to take this faith with us.

It is not easy to hold on to the vision. There have always been obstacles, and there always will be. It is never an easy thing to believe, but it is always possible.

We cannot remind ourselves too often that it is not our believing in things that makes them true. We believe them because they *are* true. Even if every Christian in the whole world were to lose his faith, that would not change *the faith.* During the 1930's, Russia instituted a massive "No God Movement." The Communist regime passed a law which stated that Jesus Christ never existed. What difference did that make *to the fact*? Denials sometimes help a cause. I am told that in Washington no one believes a rumor until it is officially denied. Our reaction to facts does not alter them as facts. Even if we had never heard of Christ's birth, and so had no reaction to it at all, that would not change the fact that in the fullness of the time the Son of God humbled Himself "and was found in fashion as a man" (Philippians 2:8).

We fail to keep the spirit of Christmas not because we do not know the Christmas story, but because we know it only in a detached and impersonal way, as we know the story of David and Goliath or Jack and the Beanstalk.

The Shepherds on the hill-slopes of Judea *accepted* the words of the heavenly messenger. "Behold, I bring *you* good tidings of great joy, which shall be to all people, for *unto you* is born this day, in the city of David, a Saviour which is Christ the Lord" (Luke 2:10f.). The simple Shepherds believed the angel. They accepted it as true that very near to them was the Saviour, who was God veiled in flesh.

The celestial lights were dimmed once more. All around them was intensely dark again. But the Shepherds had caught the spirit of Christmas. They sped with joyful haste to Bethlehem. There they proved the faithfulness of God for themselves: "And they found Mary and Joseph, and the babe lying in a manger" (Luke 2:16). God had come to them. They knew what "Emmanuel" meant. They knew why He had come. A *Saviour* was what they needed, wanted, sought and found.

* * * * *

The story says that the Shepherds "returned" (Luke 2:20). Where? They returned to their sheep. They went back to their despised daily occupation, back to their earthy, menial job, after the Divine Christmas celebrations.

How did they return? Were they disgusted because their

brief vacation was ended? Were they disgruntled at having to go back to the old drudgery? Did they carry nothing with them from Bethlehem?

"The shepherds returned, glorifying and praising God for all the things that they had heard and seen, as it was told unto them" (Luke 2:20). They had heard the announcement from heaven that the Saviour had been born. They had seen Him for themselves. He had become part of their immediate personal experience.

The Shepherds kept the spirit of Christmas. They told everybody *what had happened to them.* It was such a marvelous tale that all who heard it "wondered" (Luke 2:18).

We are born doubters. But I have yet to meet a man who doubts his own experience. If we would keep the spirit of Christmas, we must first of all experience the birth of the Christ in our own hearts.

We are told that the Wise Men went home another way. Of course they did. They had been to the Manger. They had gazed upon the Holy Child, and they had knelt in adoration before Him. They had looked into the face of God, and they had become attuned to His voice. They were thinking new thoughts, and they had a different sense of values. They had caught the spirit of Christmas, and they were determined to keep it.

They were determined to keep it at all cost. Herod had commanded them to return to him, but they disobeyed him. They risked his royal wrath to keep what they had gained. "And being warned of God in a dream that they should not return unto Herod, they departed into their own country another way" (Matthew 2:12). They followed the path of obedience to God. It is the only way to keep the spirit of Christmas.

In *The Idylls of the King,* Lord Tennyson describes the arrival of Gareth at King Arthur's city. Gareth wanted to enlist in the service of the king. An old seer accosted him and warned him of all that was involved in serving Arthur.

> *Yet take thou heed of him, for, so thou pass*
> *Beneath this archway, then wilt thou become*
> *A thrall to his enchantments, for the king*
> *Will bind thee by such vows, as is a shame*
> *A man should not be bound by, yet the which*
> *No man can keep. . . .*

But Gareth, undaunted by the seer's words, passed through the gate. He was willing to sacrifice everything to serve the king.

We have the privilege of serving the King of kings. It is not an easy task. We cannot shoulder it one day and set it aside the next. It challenges us to deny ourselves, take up the cross, and follow Him (Matthew 10:38). It is hard, but it is the only way to keep the spirit of Christmas. It is so hard that we cannot keep the spirit of Christmas unless the spirit of Christmas keep us.

Do you ever wish you had lived when Jesus was on earth? Do you long nostalgically to have shared the mystic hours of His birth? Do you feel it would have been much easier to follow Him if you had known Him in the days of His flesh?

Such desires are natural. But they are mistaken. They are based on the assumption that we are separated from Jesus today. Nothing could be further from the truth. When Jesus conquered death, He returned "in the power of His resurrection to fulfill His promise, "I am with you always" (Matthew 28:20).

He is here, closer than breathing, nearer than hands or feet. We can be just as sure that He is with us as the disciples were when they walked the dusty lanes of Palestine in His presence.

"The saints are the sinners who keep on trying," said Robert Louis Stevenson, and he was right. But he was only half right. They keep on trying — they keep the spirit of Christmas — because the Spirit of Christ keeps them. That is His work. Perseverance is the work of Sovereign Grace. We are "kept by the power of God through faith unto salvation" (1 Peter 1:5). It is to Him we pray:

Fill us with holy love,
Heal Thou our earthly pride;
Born in each lowly heart,
For ever there abide.

—Charles Coffin